THE Just Seventeen

GUIDE to being

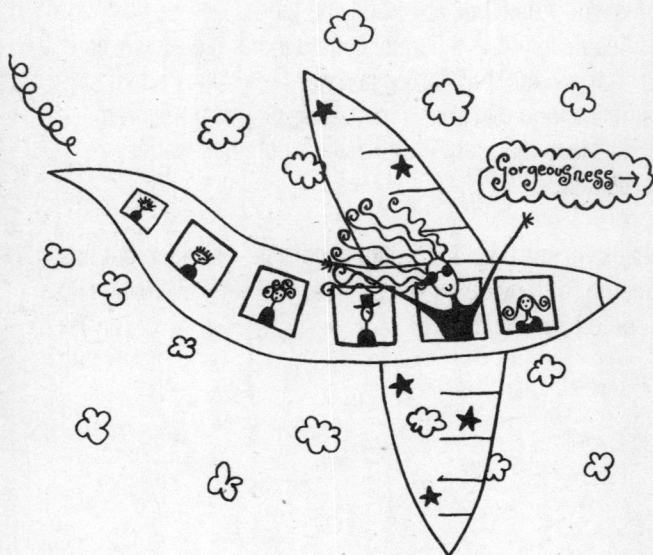

gorgeousness →

GORGEOUS

All About Adele

Award-winning journalist Adele Lovell worked for *Just Seventeen* for four fun-packed years, where she was Beauty Editor and supplier of sun-block on office days out. She is now freelance, and works for various glam magazines.

Despite being the acknowledged expert in teen beauty journalism, Adele has absolutely no journalistic qualifications and has never done a beauty course in her life. However, she is extremely adept at asking awkward questions about cosmetics, and can spot a marketing ploy at a hundred paces. Most importantly, she always puts her readers' interests first.

Adele says she was a thoroughly horrible teenager, but has made up for it by being kind, caring and sensitive ever since. Or something like that.

THE Just Seventeen GUIDE to being GORGEOUS

Adele Lovell

illustrations by Carol Morley

h

*Hodder
Children's
Books*

a division of Hodder Headline plc

Text copyright © 1996 Adele Lovell

The right of Adele Lovell to be identified as the author of the work has been asserted by her in accordance with the Copyright, Designs and Patents Act 1988.

'Just Seventeen' is a trademark of EMAP Elan
Registered Office:
1 Lincoln Court
Lincoln Road
Peterborough
PE1 2RF

Illustrations by Carol Morley

Design by Trisha Mitchell Vargas

Published by Hodder Children's Books 1996

10 9 8 7 6 5 4 3 2 1

All rights reserved. No part of this publication may be reproduced, stored in a retrieval system, or transmitted, in any form or by any means without the prior written permission of the publisher, nor to be otherwise circulated in any form of binding or cover other than that which it is published and without a similar condition being imposed on the subsequent purchaser.

ISBN 0 340 64886 4

Printed by Cox and Wyman

Hodder Children's Books
A division of Hodder Headline plc
338 Euston Road
London NW1 3BH

Contents

chapter 1

Be beautiful! Be you

...the secret of inner gorgeousness

Growing up. 'Tis weird for sure. You may feel like the same bod inside, but outside — well, when you look in the mirror it's sometimes hard to even recognise yourself. Gone is the fresh faced, vest-wearing gal you used to be, along comes...well what?

Welcome to your teen years, where there's only one certainty about the new you that you are becoming — there's no going back.

Going, going, gone are the days of deciding whether or not to pick the scabs off your knee caps; now the big issue is whether to wax or shave your legs. You stop wondering if your hair's best kept out of the way in one pony tail or two, and start contemplating a graduated bob with face-framing highlights (yep, that is a hair cut). Your favourite jeans don't fit you anymore, and when you look around for a new pair you're bombarded with pictures of stick-thin models in trews that would have been too tight when you were 10, never mind now.

wax or shave ?

wax kit

When you go to the beach you have to master the art of changing behind a towel, and the guy in the bread shop who's been calling you 'son' for the last six years starts calling you 'love' (urgh!) instead.

The boy down the road who you beat hands down at marbles turns from weedy oik to number one love god in but a matter of months. And what happens to you? You get spots, greasy hair, periods and more homework; and to top all the confusion, everyone keeps telling you that these are the best years of your life.

7

heeeeelp!

So you're growing up. You may not be totally obsessed with the rights and wrongs of mascara application, or hanker after knowing the difference between an emollient and exfoliator (by the way, one's a moisturiser and the other takes away dead skin cells). But there are few girls – or boys for that matter, but hey, they can get their own book – who wouldn't mind the odd tip or two to help them look a tad more fab. It's not that you want to be a megastar (although I'm sure you're open to offers) it's just that you want to feel downright, deep-down good about yourself.

Well, you've come to the right place for the secret of inner gorgeousness (and the outer gorgeousness which cannot fail to go with it). And it is just a few moments' reading away. You see, before you trip headlong into the confusing world of young womanhood, you need to get a few ground rules sorted out.

Which Product?

8

The most important key to surviving teenhood is to be confident in yourself and your abilities. That doesn't mean pretending to be the cleverest, most attractive person in the world but it does mean being aware of your own potential and believing in it. And don't let anyone put you off or put you down.

Be really positive; believe that you look good, that you're intelligent, and that good things are going to happen. If something is getting you down it's time for some positive thinking – mental virtual reality without the silly goggles. Replace all the bad vibes with good ones by imagining your problem is long gone and that instead of a sad bad ending, it had a 'happy ever after' ending.

Love your body. So what if you're no supermodel – your body is still an awesome, amazing thing worthy of all the care and attention you can lavish upon it. Keep fit, eat well, dress to flatter your figure, and be proud of yourself.

Don't believe the hype. There's more to being beautiful than wearing the right lipstick or choosing a certain shampoo. Looking good and feeling good only come about when you look after your whole self, inside and out.

9

A Different Hairstyle

Monday   Tuesday   Wednesday   Thursday

Understand the physical changes you are going through during puberty so that you feel comfortable with them. This book helps by explaining what's what, and lets you into the complicated (except it's not) world of hair, make-up and skin care that's part of becoming a young woman. It also helps to have someone to confide in, be it a friend who's going through the same thing, or an older bod who's already been there, done that, and lived to tell the tale.

Teen years are about discovering the new you, and experimenting with how you look. So try every make-up combination you can think of, and style your hair a different way for every day of the week, not because that's the right and proper thing to do (you've got the rest of your life for that), but because it's good fun seeing how you look. Enjoy your new self!

Don't take yourself too seriously. In many respects teen years are a dress rehearsal for the rest of your adult life; now's the time you get your first boyfriend, start going out on your own, maybe get your first job. There are lots of new things to experience and no one expects you to get everything right first time. So go ahead and buy those high heels only to find they are the most uncomfortable things you've ever had within a six mile radius of your body. Dye your hair

10

Every Day
Friday Saturday Sunday.

blonde and realise it doesn't suit you. Drop half a box of tampons all over the pavement while trying to find your purse at a crowded bus stop. Wanna know how to cope? Laugh about it. Tee hee.

★ Make a list of your good points and look at it every time you're feeling miserable. Include everything you can think of – from the highly individual style with which you have decorated your bedroom to the wondrousness of your hair. Don't stop writing until you've thought of at least 20 things and feel free to add more things whenever you like.

Good Points
* Blue Eyes
* Happy face
* Nice Hands
* Good Cook
* Lots of friends
* Strong
* Good at o·l·y
* long Hair
* Good Skin
* ∼∼∼
* ∼∼∼

Ignore people who tease you or call you names because you may look different. They don't do it to get at you (although it probably seems that way), they do it to make themselves feel better. The fact that they have to sink so low to feel good shows that they've got lots of problems, and that you don't need to hang around with them any longer.

11

★ Don't get obsessed with the way you look. No one is perfect and although there's nothing wrong with trying to make the best of yourself, it shouldn't become the most important thing in your life. If you spend more time styling your hair than you spend on your homework or hanging out with your mates then something's not quite right.

🌀 And finally, read this book. It covers everything from pubic hair to getting a perm, and lets you into all the secrets you need to know in order to plain-sail your way to being a sussed young woman of a somewhat gorgeous nature; for this is what you surely are.

dead easy quiz

Think you're a creature of ultimate confidence who can't fail to be one cool teenager? Or does the thought of growing up have you hiding behind your teddy bear? Do this quiz and see.

1 A boy you like just asked you out. How do you feel?

A Not in the least surprised. All the boys fancy you, after all.

B Really flattered and a bit relieved; you were beginning to think that you'd have to ask him out.

C Totally gob-smacked and utterly flattered. Supposing you go out and he decides he doesn't like you?

2 You've got a split end. What do you do?

A Have a barney with the hairdresser; how dare he/she fail to snip it off.

B Anxiously search for others, then make a hairdressing appointment.

C Blame your parents for giving birth to such a weak-haired individual (ahem), don a hat and generally feel glum.

3 Your armpits are smelly. What's the next step?

A Pretend that it's someone else; it couldn't possibly be you.

B Wash, apply deodorant and change your clothes, but worry that it will happen again.

C Construct a large perimeter fence around your body and erect a sign saying 'B.O. zone: enter at own risk.'

4 'You're a 34B,' says the shop assistant. Is she referring to:

A Your average homework grade.

B Your bra size.

C Your blood group.

5 Your make-up bag is full of...

A Loads of stuff that makes you look divinely sexy.

B A bit of colour to enhance your looks; although you're not sure if the colours are right.

C A few scraps that your big sister had finished with.

...how did you score?

m⊙stly As

You are packed full of confidence, which is always a good thing. But don't assume that you know everything already and don't need help or guidance through those potentially rocky teen years. True confidence only comes about when you are at one with your self, your body, and the changes that are happening to it. Keep reading this book and you'll be well on your way.

mostly Bs

You've got your head screwed on for sure, but you still feel a bit insecure about what is happening to you. What you really want are a few facts about your new self, and reassurance that you are on the right track. That's what this book is here for!

mostly Cs

The change from child to fully-fledged woman is making you feel very nervous; you really aren't sure if you'll be able to cope. You need to accept that worrying isn't the solution: life goes on despite your anxieties, and things usually turn out much better than you expect them to. Use this book for guidance and you'll feel more confident about the future.

chapter 2

Your Body

...the one you don't recognise anymore

our body changes more during your teen years than at any other time in your adult life. While the most obvious physical changes occur during your early teens, they continue right through until you are about 18. Although these changes are completely natural, it can seem like they are happening at an alarming rate, especially if you don't feel ready emotionally. If you feel out of step with all the transformations your body is undergoing, don't worry and don't be embarrassed.

Sooner or later, and it is usually sooner, you and your body will be happily reunited, completely in accord and totally in step.
The best way to cope with, accept and like your new self is to understand what is happening. As soon as you are in control of the low-down, the rest is a walk in the park. Easy.

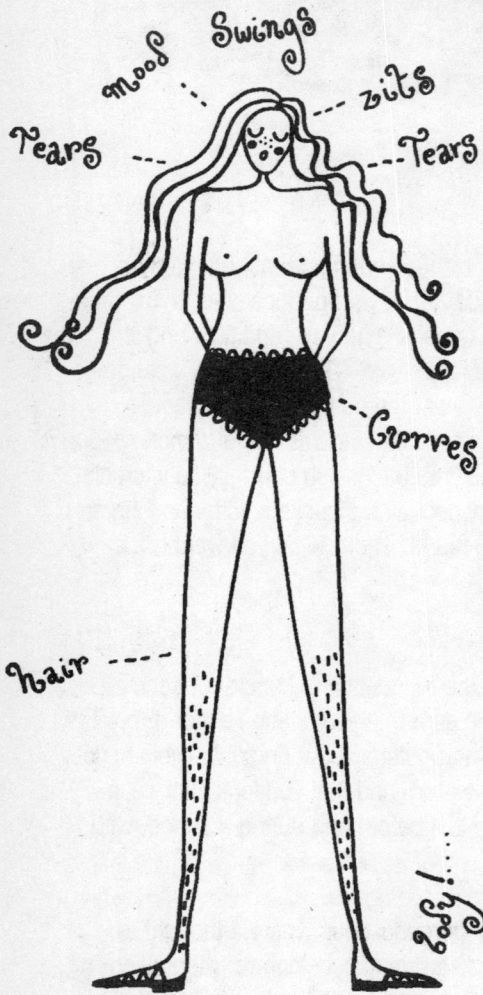

The story so far: you are leaving kids' stuff behind and are approaching at the speed of light – roll of drums and loud applause – adulthood. Your body and your feelings are changing as your sex hormones roll into action. These hormones orchestrate the new-look, new-thinking you. As if radical mood swings, tears and tempers weren't enough to cope with, you also have to learn to love and manage a new curvy body, periods, zits, smelly armpits, hair, hair and more hair. Time for some crucial detail.

Swings

mood

zits

Tears

Tears

Curves

hair

I don't recognise my body!

periods

The most obvious and important change that takes place is that your periods start at any time between the ages of 9 and 16, and suddenly the previously unexplored aisle 12 at Sainsbury's becomes real important. You quite rightly want the best sanitary protection around. Being confident that no tell-tale smear is going to make you a wallflower and stop you doing all the things you normally do is crucial. So go on, read all the labels, inspect all the packets, loiter as long as you like in aisle 12 until you've found exactly what you want, be it sanitary towels or tampons.

But good health – the foundation of knock-out good looks – means that you have to make sure that you change either a towel or tampon regularly, that you are scrupulous about personal hygiene (lots of mild, unperfumed soap and water), and that you look after your inner gorgeousness, especially just before and during a period, with all the care you can lavish.

And while we are talking about gorgeousness, spare a thought to keeping the world gorgeous too, by being considerate when disposing of sanitary towels and tampons. If the sign on the loo door says 'Please use the bin provided' – use it. Even at home it is recommended that you avoid shoving things down the loo and

18

flushing 10 times (they don't disappear forever, you know). Instead, wrap up used towels and tampons securely and dispose of them with the household rubbish.

PMS

Coping with your period is actually very easy. It's the side effects that go with it that can make life so much more difficult. These symptoms are known as PMS (pre-menstrual syndrome) and they include spots, greasy hair, oily skin, stomach cramps, swollen and tender breasts and nipples, swollen ankles and fingers, a bloated feeling, and a real down-in-the-dumps mood swing. They occur just before your period, and some suffer more than others. Some (bless 'em) are never affected.

When you first start to experience these symptoms it can really catch you out, but try not to feel too glum. As your menstrual cycle becomes more regular you'll be able to predict your off-days. That doesn't mean you can spend PMS days in bed hugging a teddy and a hot water bottle, eating chocolate biscuits and watching daytime TV. Imagine how many good things you'd miss if you removed yourself from the social calendar for a couple of days

Greasy Hair

oily Skin

MARCH
1 8 15 22
2 9 16 23
3 10 17 24
4 11 18 25
5 12 19 26
6 13 20 ⬛ ← Due.
7 14 21 28

Swollen Breasts

Stomach ache

PAIN KILLER

Down in the Dumps.

Swollen Ankles

19

each month. So try these measures which are both practical and effective and will keep you out there where it's happening.

1 A week before your period, up your intake of fruit, leafy green vegetables, eggs, cheese, meat and fish or pulses and beans; the nutrients they contain will help ease PMS symptoms.

2 Throughout the month make sure you eat lots of wholemeal bread, cereals and bananas, all of which are high in Vitamin B6. Other minerals, vitamins and extracts thought to help are Evening Primrose oil, vitamins E and C as well as zinc, selenium, magnesium and calcium. If your diet is balanced (see chapter 3), there is no need for these supplements, so always seek advice first. Maybe your diet just needs a tweak.

3 To make up for the iron your body loses during your period eat lots of iron-rich foods like peas, liver, spinach and unsalted nuts.

4 Cut down on salty foods like crisps; the salt content makes your body retain water and makes you feel more bloated.

5 Exercise can help relieve muscle cramps, but don't go overboard – you might just replace period cramp with aching muscles.

6 Essential oil, available from health food shops, can also work; camomile and lavender are good and don't cost too much. Make sure you get advice from a trained aromatherapist on how to use them (ask at the shop where you buy them); if you don't know what you're doing, essential oils can be ineffective, and could even be dangerous.

7 If the pain is too much to bear ask your chemist to recommend a pain-killing drug, being quite specific about what you want it for. Pain-killers can be extremely effective and work very quickly so that you can get on with your life. Follow dosage and duration of use instructions to the letter.

body
shape

our body will change a lot during puberty. The more obvious changes are the development of your breasts (did I hear a hooray?), the growth of pubic hair and armpit hair (in fact a little hairier everywhere), and fat on your hips and buttocks. Your face will become fuller, your pelvis widens giving you a curvaceous shape, your genitals grow slightly, and your voice deepens a little as well. And you thought that only happened to boys.

Of course, these changes don't happen overnight – they occur at different rates for different people, and can take up to six years; you don't stop growing until you're 18.

The body shape you're in

Body shapes fall into three categories – ectomorph, mesmomorph and endomorph, and you inherit yours from your parents. Very few people are perfect examples of one body type but you'll probably have more characteristics from one group than any other. There is no 'right' or 'wrong' body shape – each one is as healthy and potentially attractive as any other.

Ectomorphs are tall and lean, probably small chested with small hips and bum, long bones, and not much muscle. They tend not to put on weight easily.

Body Types

Ectomorph   Mesmomorph   Endomorph

Mesmomorphs are curvy with a definite bust, waist and hip shape, with wide shoulders tapering down to slimmer hips. They are muscular with medium to large bones and don't put on weight easily.

Endomorphs are short, muscly and naturally rounded with wide hips and heavy bodies. They tend to put on weight very easily.

Endomorphic mesmomorphs are voluptuous, with medium to large bones and a tendency to put on weight.

Mesmomorphic ectomorphs are lean but quite muscular with a definite bust and hip shape. They do not gain weight easily.

looking good

he secret of looking good and feeling happy about your body shape is to accept and like what you are, and then enhance it. Try not to spend your waking hours battling with the way you look through dieting; there's so much more to life and being happy than worrying over a packet of diet biscuits, the bathroom scales and a calorie counter.

23

Next time you go out to buy a new outfit or flip through the pages of a magazine ogling catwalk creations, keep these ideas in your mind:

Dark colours tone down areas that you don't want to emphasise.

Bright colours grab attention to the areas you do like.

Large bold patterns exaggerate a large figure, while small and medium prints will flatter.

Thin vertical stripes make you look taller and thinner but the wider the stripe, the more 'boxy' you tend to look. Just remember what they make tents of – they don't call them 'big tops' for nothing.

Horizontal stripes make you look curvy and more voluptuous. The wider the stripe, the greater the effect.

Stripes

Vertical   or   Horizontal ?

★ If you have large hips focus attention upwards by wearing scarves, hats and dramatic jewellery. Avoid cropped jackets and pockets on skirts and trousers.

🌀 Shirt pockets will draw attention to your bust.

★ It is best to match tights to the colour of your shoes; this will make your legs look longer.

🌀 Clothes with a fitted waist or belt draw attention to your upper body, make your legs look longer, and your breasts look bigger.

★ Clothes with a straight cut tend to emphasise hips and elongate your body. These clothes are easy to wear and have an androgynous look.

🌀 Clothes that are too tight make bigger girls look larger, and make skinny girls look thinner.

★ Baggy clothes make large busts and hips look larger, and a skinny body look even leaner.

Baggy

Tight fit

When you buy jeans, shop around for the

pair that flatters your figure. Originally, jeans were only designed for men, and were therefore 'men-shaped'. This was fine for women who had small hips and little bottom to speak of, but verged on the edge of disaster for anyone with a more curvaceous, womanly shape. Thankfully, it is now possible to buy jeans that are designed for all sorts of body shapes: big hips, long legs, tiny waists, high waists, generous buttocks etc. Specialist jeans shops with vast stocks will give you the best choice.

Clothes that fit

well are most flattering. You

may want to be a size 12, but if size 14 fits you better then you do yourself no favours by buying the smaller size and thinking you can diet into it. It will make you miserable and drain the finances. Much better to have an outfit that you can wear over and over, knowing that it fits you really well and that you look good in it, and boy-oh-boy don't you know it.

Choose clothes

that you feel comfortable in over stuff that makes a huge fashion statement but has the comfort level of a packet of drawing pins.

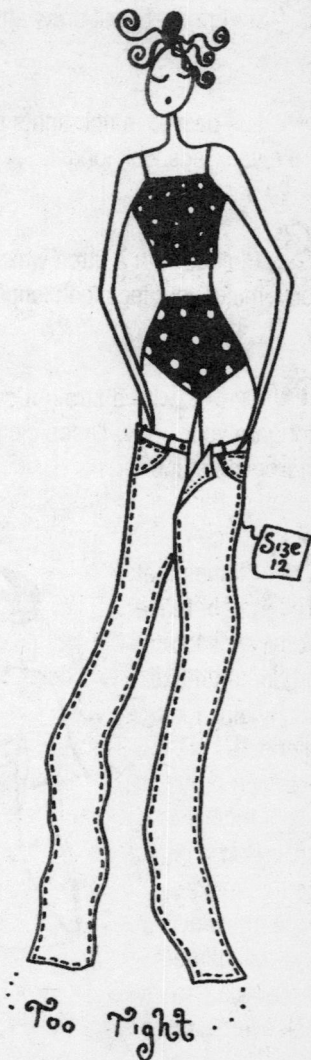

Size 12

Too Tight

breasts

Breast size is mostly dependent upon your genes and you will probably have a bust that is similar to your mother's. The amount of fat on your body also affects bust size, as this is one area where the body deposits fat.

Your breasts will develop as your body evolves through puberty, so just because your friend's bust is bigger than yours, or vice versa, doesn't mean it will always be that way.

There is no ideal breast size. Speak to 'big girls' and they will moan about being called names, being unable to run for the bus, and the limited choice of really nice affordable underwear.

Girls with a small chest complain of not casting a shadow in profile and of a nonexistent cleavage. However they look brilliant in vest tops and strappy clothes, and have probably never missed a bus in their life.

By the way, it's quite normal to have one breast or even a nipple that is slightly larger than the other one. Sometimes their size evens out as you grow, but if it doesn't don't worry – there's nothing wrong and it's very rarely noticeable.

27

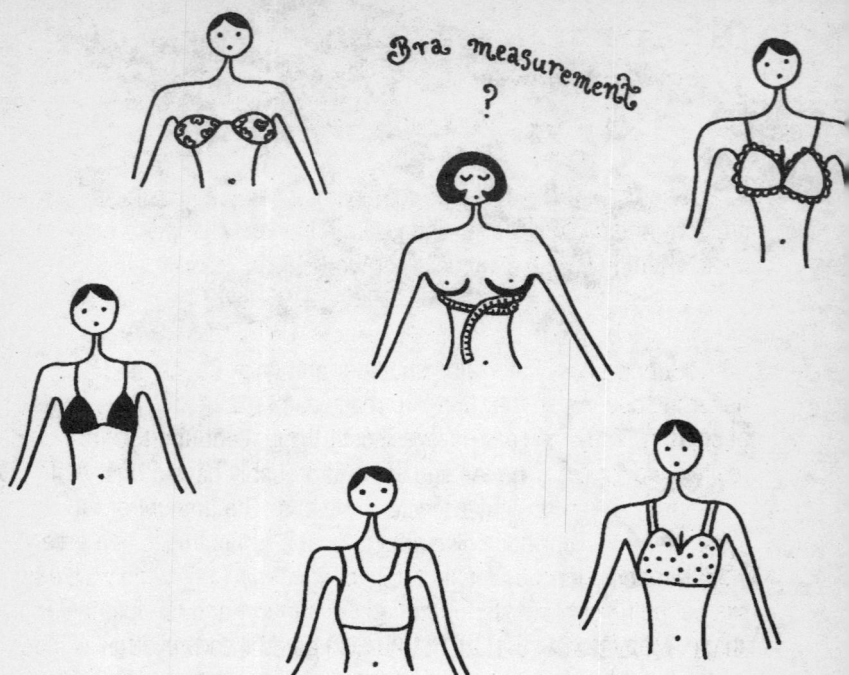

Bra measurement ?

Buying a bra

Once you get out of your vest-wearing years you'll need to buy a bra. Go for a fitting as soon as you see a change in your breast size, even though it may be very slight. It's really important that you visit a store where trained fitters can assess your size; guesswork on your behalf isn't good enough.

A well-fitting bra is essential for girls with a large bust because it offers extra support. Breasts, being mostly fat, don't contain any muscle, so unless you provide some scaffolding, gravity will take over and your breasts will be heavy and uncomfortable. Smaller-breasted girls also benefit from wearing a good bra, because it stops your breasts moving around too much and can give that extra shape and definition so desired.

There are several types of bra to choose from

✺ Sports bras are designed to minimise bounce, maximise support, and allow sweat to evaporate. They are cut specially to avoid chaffing on the shoulders and underarms.

★ Support bras have wide shoulder and back straps, and a generous cup cut so that they are really comfortable and give loads of support. They may not be the sexiest things ever, but they are really good for everyday wear.

✺ Underwired bras contain a thin piece of shaped metal wire that sits beneath your breasts, offering extra support and an uplifting shape. Many people are put off them because they think they will be uncomfortable; in fact they are very comfortable if the size is right.

★ Soft bras are usually made from a light fabric using a softer cut than support bras. They give a more natural shape but less support, so they're best for smaller busts.

✺ Balcony bras and push-up bras are 'special occasion' items that are designed to enhance your cleavage. They look great but only wear them if you feel happy sporting a pair of very noticeable breasts.

★ Seamless, flesh-coloured bras are designed to be worn under sheer clothes or very clingy numbers.

Well-fitting Bra

Going for a fitting

Go to a department store or lingerie shop where you can be measured by a trained female member of staff who will be very discreet, professional and quick.

She will measure you around and beneath your breasts. The measurement beneath your breasts is used to calculate the size of your rib cage – usually 32, 34 or 36 inches. The measurement around your breasts is used to work out your cup size – the bigger the difference between the two measurements, the larger cup size you need. Cup sizes range from A to F.

Some fitters assess your breast size simply by looking. It can be a bit weird standing topless in front of a complete stranger while she stares at your breasts, but try not to be phased by it – she won't be embarrassed, so you shouldn't be either.

You will be given a selection of bras to try – some will fit better than others, depending upon their cut. It's important to adjust the shoulder straps correctly. Too loose and you're forever hoiking them up, too tight and it's sheer agony. Go for the one that fits you best rather than the one you happen to like the look of; your everyday bra should be there for support, not to make a fashion statement.

You will need to be measured

every six months through puberty. This is because your body size can change a lot within this time, and bras lose their shape and support with time and repeated washing.

your underwear

...and your clothes

nless you are making a big, bold fashion statement, underwear is meant to be precisely that – worn under your clothes, where it remains invisible. Because of the cut of certain garments, you may have to have a selection of differently cut pants to avoid the dreaded VPL. If you have a VPL it's time to change your knickers. No, it's not a scary medical condition, it's your Visible Panty Line (VBL, of course, stands for Visible Bra Line). This line shows through your clothes where the edges of your underwear lie against your skin. Not only can VPL be embarrassing, it ruins the look of your clothes.

Gym knickers   French knickers   Briefs

Panty line up

🌀 G-strings look like instruments of torture, but in reality allow you to wear the tightest jeans without a hint of an unwelcome line. G-strings feature a high waist band, small front section and reduced gusset, and a thin length of fabric in place of the normal back section. They are, surprisingly, a lot more comfortable than they look and can be the difference between looking smooth, streamlined and gorgeous in your clothes or looking rumpled.

⭐ French knickers are loose-fitting, high-waisted pants that do not have elastic around the legs. They are extremely comfortable under loose fitting clothes but tend to rumple under tighter garments.

🌀 Gym knickers, with a high elasticated waistband and lower cut legs have undergone something of a fashion revival. They can crease beneath tight clothes, but are very comfortable and perfect under short skirts if you do not wish to reveal all to the world on a windy day.

Aside from G-strings, most women find that the larger their pants the more flattering they are beneath their clothes. Beware of the skimpy, hip-hugging type that sit on the fatty areas of your hip and bottom; they are the biggest VPL culprits. Much better to chose athletic-looking, high-waisted, high-cut leg pants that sit smoothly on the skin. Plain cotton is the most versatile and the fairest on your skin; patterned knickers with ribbons and bows are more likely to show.

hair

ubic and armpit hair first appears during puberty and it is thought that it prevents chafing in these areas where the skin is very sensitive and prone to rubbing. Hair, wherever it is, also guides sweat from the pores to the air where it can evaporate. Hair elsewhere on your body – yes, even your toes – may also become darker and thicker during puberty.

The fact that many women choose to remove and shape their pubic hair is due to fashionably high-cut knickers, swimming costumes and G-strings; however, many cultures around the world never give pubic hair a second thought, so if you don't want to remove it, don't feel you have to.

What to remove

Legs – all the hair from your knees downwards, and don't forget hair grows on the back of your legs.

Armpits – all the hair.

34

Groin – remove hair from your bikini line only. This means removing the hair that shows when you wear pants or high-cut costumes. Don't remove hair any closer to your genitalia as pubic hair helps protect this very sensitive area.

De-fuzzestation methods

★ Razor

This is the easiest, quickest and cheapest method, and is suitable for all areas. Hair reappears within two or three days, but contrary to the myth, it will not grow back thicker – it just looks that way because of the angle at which the razor cuts the hair.

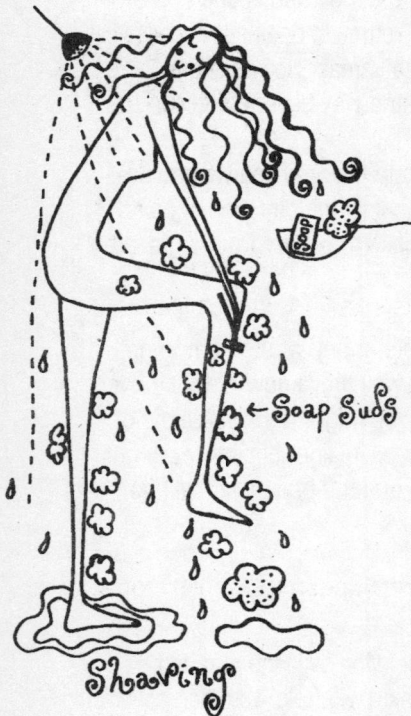

Soap Suds

Shaving

Step 1 Exfoliate by gently rubbing in a handful of sea salt. This will avoid in-growing hairs which appear as small red bumps.

Step 2 Make sure you use a clean razor (never use anyone else's), and shave after a bath when the hairs will be softer and easier to cut.

Step 3 Cover the area to be shaved in a thick layer of mild moisturising soap suds, and shave against the direction of hair growth, holding the skin taut where necessary.

Step 4 Rinse and dry your skin, then apply unperfumed moisturiser to soothe it.

☺ Depilatory creams

Good for legs and bikini lines, although you'll need different products for each. A bikini line cream is formulated for sensitive skin and will be less likely to cause irritation.

Depilatory creams work by dissolving the hair. Sounds horrendous, I know, but it is perfectly safe if you follow the instructions on the pack really carefully. Once the cream is applied (sometimes a rather messy job) it takes a few minutes for it to do its stuff. Hair regrowth will appear in about 5-7 days.

★ Waxing

Waxing works by pulling the hair out at the root, and is one of the most effective de-fuzz methods as hair regrowth does not occur for at least two weeks. Waxing is suitable for all areas. Hot waxing is normally done at a beauty salon while strip wax is perfect for DIY.

DIY Smooth the sticky wax strip on to the area you wish to de-fuzz and then quickly pull it off, going against the direction of hair growth. It feels a bit like removing a week-old plaster from a grazed knee. Ouch!

Because waxing is a little uncomfortable, many women opt to go to a beauty salon to have it done; that way they know it will be over and done with as quickly as possible. You might think you'll die of embarrassment when it comes to your bikini line, but it's really not so bad – you keep your underwear on and the beautician will be very discreet.

☺ Sugaring

Sugaring involves spreading a sugary solution over the area to be treated, having previously dusted your skin with talc. You then cover with cotton sugaring strips and yank them back against the direction of hair growth, thereby removing the hair. The cotton sugaring strips are reusable and the complete kits are available at most chemists. Hair regrowth will not occur for at least two weeks. Sugaring is not only easier than waxing, it is also less painful.

Facial hair

We all grow very fine hairs above our top lip, almost unnoticeable unless the hair is dark. In health terms there is nothing to worry about (no, you're not turning into a man), but you may feel self-conscious and wish it wasn't there. There are four ways to keep facial hair under check.

Facial hair bleaching cremes are very effective so long as you follow the instructions and timings to the letter. They do not remove the hair, but simply lighten it. Don't try lightening facial hair with any other type of hair dye as you risk burning or irritating the delicate skin on your face.

Facial hair depilatory creams work by dissolving the hair. Make sure it is a product specifically for your face.

Facial waxing treatments are available at a beauty salon.

Electrolysis is a permanent hair removal method, but it takes several sessions to remove all the hair, can be uncomfortable and also quite expensive. You must go to a qualified beauty therapist for this treatment.

The final word: if you don't want to de-fuzz, then don't.

perspiration

When you were a kid you never gave a second thought to the lather of sweat you ran up playing in the park, but once puberty comes along perspiration becomes a whole new ball game – you become aware of it and so do your close friends. During puberty your body starts to emit a type of sweat which, if left unchecked, can be really smelly.

At puberty the apocine glands in your armpits and groin become active. It is thought that the subtle smell of their secretions acts as a 'magnet' to members of the opposite sex, but the effect is so subtle it is not likely to cause men to drop at your feet, begging to sniff your pits. It is the action of the skin's bacteria over a period of hours upon this sweat which causes BO or body odour, which instead of acting like a magnet tends to make people keep their distance. But as in all things human, everyone is different. Some folks sweat bending down to tie their shoelaces, others do a half marathon with not a drop to show for it.

Armpit hygiene

The best way to avoid BO is to wash regularly – twice a day, morning and evening, is ideal. You should also wear anti-perspirant deodorant during the day. Deodorants work by blocking some of the pores in your armpits so you sweat less, and by masking smells as they start to develop. Choose either roll-on, pump spray, aerosol or stick variants – they are all equally effective.

If you have sensitive skin, use anti-perspirants that are fragrance-free or, even better, specially formulated for sensitive skin. These products are also good to use on recently shaved underarms when the skin tends to be sensitive.

Clothes that are stained with sweat tend to pick up a stale smell, so it's best to change anything that comes into contact with your armpits daily, shirts and T-shirts especially. That's why most of the adult population have developed a secret habit of sniffing the armpits of their clothes as they dress. Strange but true, dear reader.

De-fuzzing your armpits may help you to stay fresher, but it is no substitute for washing regularly or applying anti-perspirant deodorant.

Try not to worry about being smelly – if you follow these guidelines you won't have a problem. However in hot weather it may be worth having a wash and reapplying deodorant at lunch time or after sport.

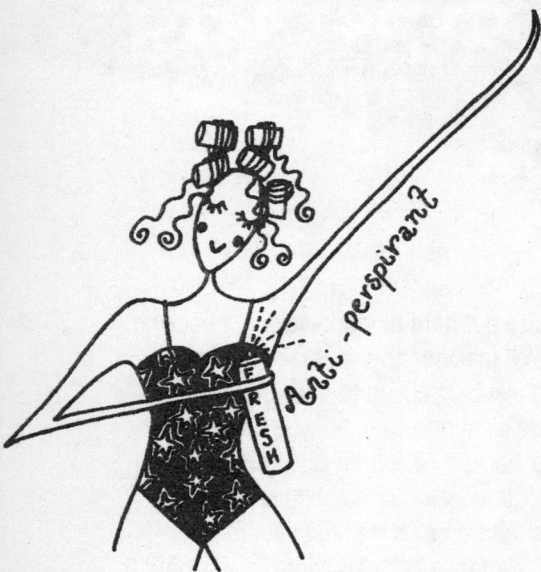

Groin hygiene

The big difference here is that you don't wear deodorant around your groin. This is because there is a very delicate balance of bacteria in this area – which is actually there to help keep it clean. Highly fragranced 'feminine hygiene' products which are formulated to keep the groin area fresh can upset this mini-eco system and cause an itchy irritation, although many women can use them without problem. To keep the crotch fresh – wash daily with unperfumed soap and water, wear clean cotton-gussetted pants, and then let mother nature do the rest.

all-over body pampering

hen you're not hard at work waxing, checking for VPLs or making sure your diet is super-healthy, you will be pleased to hear that some beauty products exist only to make you feel nice all-over. An indulgent, fragrance-packed bath time is a treat that women have a monopoly of; just check out the shop shelves groaning under the weight of bath cremes and bubbles for proof. To help you sort the bubbles from the...bubbles, here is an at-a-glance guide to bathing in style.

🌀 Bubble bath: not only does it fill your bath with bubbles, it softens the water and even smells nice. Some can dry your skin, so choose a formulation that moisturises too.

⭐ Moisturising creme bath: a skin softening treat that stops your skin from drying out in the bath water. As with any fragranced product, beware of overusing them; they can cause irritation.

🌀 Bath oil: liquid or oil-filled capsules which disperse in the water leaving a moisturising sheen on your skin. Those containing essential oils offer therapeutic benefits. You can buy ready mixed 'relaxing' and 'reviving' formulations, but to find out about the more specialised treatments talk to an experienced aromatherapist.

★ All of the above make your skin feel good, but they don't actually clean it. Well, what did you get in the bath for after all? For a good old-fashioned rub-a-dub you need a good old-fashioned cake of soap or cleansing bar. Soap is made from animal and vegetable fats, and cleansing bars contain synthetic detergents made from petroleum derivatives. The bonus of cleansing bars is that they leave no scum around the bath. Other than that, there is little difference between them.

◎ You can also use liquid wash-off body cleansers (for use in the bath) or shower gels (for use in the shower, funnily enough). They both contain synthetic detergents.

★ Although soap makes an excellent cleanser, it can leave your skin feeling dry. That's why you should follow up your bath or shower with an application of body lotion.

◎ Moisturising body lotions are used after bathing and help keep your skin soft and stop the dryness that soaking in the bath can encourage. Your shins, elbows and knees – which contain fewer sebaceous glands than other parts of your body and so are most prone to dryness – will benefit the most. If you have sensitive skin choose an unperfumed lotion.

★ If you have a favourite perfume it is often possible to 'layer' it on your skin, using bath products from the same range. If you choose to use matching bath creme, soap, deodorant, talc, body lotion and perfume it can turn out rather expensive, but you'll be sure to smell rather heavenly.

◎ The temperature of your bath or shower water is really

42

important. Warm water is relaxing, soothing and less likely to dry your skin than a too hot bath. The 'elbow' test will tell you if water temperature is right.

⭐ A too hot bath removes the skin's own moisturising sebum, so that it feels dry and itchy. Quick, cool showers are very refreshing, and so long as the water isn't actually mountain stream cold they do not require a sharp intake of breath as you step in.

Don't overdo it! Soaking in the bath, adorned in
scented bubbles for an hour may be fabulous; but don't make a habit of it. Skin can become oversensitive and dry if you bathe too long, too often, especially if you use a lot of perfumed products. To be on the safe side, have a luxuriating soak every other day, with a simple soap and flannel wash on days between.

chapter 3

Why you don't need to diet

...healthy girls have more fun

Unfortunately, our culture has very rigid ideas of what are the 'right' and 'wrong' shapes for a woman's body. These ideals have heaps more to do with fashion than with health, but sadly their influence is deeply ingrained. You may feel pressured into trying to attain a 'perfect figure' even though achieving it may be bad for your health, or develop into an obsession.

Other cultures in the world don't share our preoccupation with thinness. In areas of Africa the 'perfect' woman is one who is obese, and some tribes deliberately fatten their women. This may sound bizarre to us, but think how our obsession with dieting and being skinny must seem to them.

Having a 'good figure' is really a lucky coincidence – where an inherited body shape just happens to correspond to today's fashion. However, it's not easy to shrug your shoulders and dismiss your 'unfashionable' shape in a culture that goes on and on about being thin. It's a predicament not made any easier during puberty when your body is constantly changing. But dismissive you must be. The amount you eat and exercise can alter your appearance and affect your health, but you can't change your basic shape (see Chapter 2).

The secret of being a truly attractive person has nothing to do with your dimensions. Intelligence, personality, confidence and social skills (like how well you get on with people) all count far more when it comes to being a happy and therefore an attractive person. You might not believe this when you're looking in the mirror and a supermodel isn't staring back, but physical appearance is just the icing on the cake. The stuff of real and everlasting gorgeousness is self-esteem, pure and simple.

why teen dieting is so bad...

ating well — as opposed to dieting — is very important for everyone. If the purpose of eating food is to fuel your body then it is easy to see why it's important to make sure that most of what you eat is good for you.

Unless you are unhealthily overweight, teen dieting is probably the worst thing you can do to your growing body. Your body needs lots and lots of energy in order to develop strong bones, muscles and internal organs. And where does energy come from? Food. So while you're fretting over whether or not to eat that extra slice of toast, your body is screaming out for every good nutrient it can get.

One of the minerals that you could be short of is iron. Some recent studies suggest that the vast majority of teenage girls are iron deficient, and it is in part due to the blood lost during a period. But other factors can also contribute: excess coffee and tea, for example.

Iron is an essential mineral for growth, resistance to disease and energy production. The outer signs of iron deficiency are brittle hair, lengthwise ridges on the nails, excessive tiredness and poor skin colour. You can get sufficient iron in your diet if you regularly

essential

eat green leafy vegetables such as spinach, plus fish, eggs, red meat, poultry, whole grains, cereals, almonds, avocados, kidney and lima beans, parsley, peaches, tofu, yoghurt and dried fruits. And you thought I was going to suggest all sorts of awful food, didn't you?

★ Another nutrient that is essential to teen health is calcium, good sources of which are dairy products, green leafy vegetables, almonds, carob (the chocolate you have when you're not eating chocolate), oats, fish, sunflower and sesame seeds. Calcium helps to strengthen your bones as they grow, which is not just important for now but also for later in your life. Calcium aids muscle growth and prevents – wait for it – muscle cramps. Goodbye period pain (well, some of it at least).

◎ Right now your body is very efficient at absorbing calcium but as you get older it won't be able to obtain enough from food. A possible consequence of this is a condition called osteoporosis which can set in at the menopause, leaving you with very weak and brittle bones. Eat properly now and you'll build strong bones that will resist this weakening. Don't make the mistake of thinking you can do something about it later.

...and eating well is so good

🌀 Eat three meals a day. Your body will work best if you have frequent, small meals rather than eating a load in one go, or – even worse – skipping meals.

⭐ Make sure your diet is high in fibre and low in fat. Fibre helps you go to the loo with absolute and necessary regularity (it's all glamour, for sure). Easiest places to find fibre: wholemeal bread and breakfast cereals.

🌀 Don't try to cut fat out of your diet completely. Although too much is not good for your heart or your waistline, you need some to stay healthy. This is because some vitamins, such as A and D, are soluble in fat, so without it you may become deficient. Secondly, some polyunsaturated fatty acids are needed to maintain cell membranes and to produce vital substances within your body.

⭐ Fats that come from animals – butter, lard and full fat milk, for example – are the ones to avoid because your body cannot digest them properly and makes potentially harmful cholesterol from them. These 'saturated fats' are hard at room temperature. Vegetable-based fats such as vegetable oil, olive oil and sunflower oil are good to eat in

48

moderation. These are known as monounsaturated or polyunsaturated fats and they are liquid at room temperature. They tend to reduce cholesterol levels.

Aim to have a balanced diet. Every day you should have five servings of fruit or veg (preferably fresh, raw and crunchy), a serving of meat or a meat substitute, and lots of milk (skimmed or semi-skimmed is best), pulses, beans and whole grains.

Drink lots of water to help your body to function properly. Aim to have six to eight glasses of water a day in winter, then up it to ten glasses a day in summer when you sweat more. It's especially important to drink lots of water during exercise to keep your body temperature down. Don't wait until you feel thirsty – that's your body's way of saying you've already gone too long without water.

You can buy special isotonic drinks to take before or after sport. Their most essential ingredient is water, which replaces body fluids used during your workout. They also contain salt to help your body absorb the water efficiently and to replace the minerals you lose as you sweat, and carbohydrates to give you energy. Isotonic means that the composition of the drink allows it be absorbed by your body at the same rate as water. Pretty clever, eh?

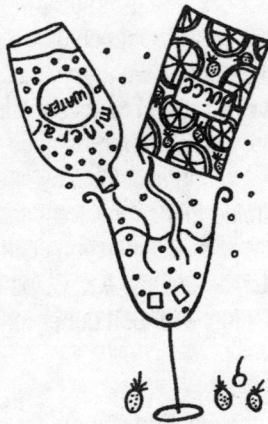

The best thirst quencher of all is fruit juice mixed with mineral water. What could be easier?

49

★ Watch your intake of 'rush foods', especially when you're feeling tired. Often the reason we crave coffee, chocolate or fizzy drinks is because of the immediate energy rush from the caffeine or sugar content. Cravings like this are your body's way of trying to cheat. Unfortunately, the energy rush is short-lived, and afterwards you feel even more tired. It's much better to eat simple carbohydrates like pasta, potatoes, fruit, veg, beans and wholegrain bread. These foods release their energy slowly, giving you far more staying power.

Start every day with fresh fruit – on its own or added to breakfast cereal. Fruit acts like a digestive vacuum cleaner, cleansing the system for everything that is to follow.

bite

Watch how much salt you consume. Although you need some salt to stay healthy, most of us eat around twenty times too much of the stuff. Salt can cause fluid retention, so cutting down can make a big difference if you suffer from PMS. Many natural foods contain salt – bread, milk, cream, cheese, butter and meat for instance, so reducing intake isn't that easy. Where you can avoid it is by not eating salty crisps and nuts, bacon and tinned foods (check the label – some are now salt-free). Never add salt to food when you cook, and certainly don't sprinkle it over your meal before you eat. Chips may never be the same again, but hey, you'll feel so much better for it.

★ Sugar makes food yummy for sure, but has no nutritional value, is high in calories and rots your teeth so give it a miss as often as possible. However, pushing away a plate of biscuits and turning your nose up at chocolate bars isn't the end of the story; many convenience foods – for instance breakfast cereals – have sugar in them so you need to read food labels carefully.

Almost five per cent of the UK population are vegetarians, and this figure rises to eleven per cent among teenagers. People give up meat for all sorts of reasons: some do it in support of animal rights, others feel that a meat-based diet isn't very healthy, while some stop because they simply don't like meat.

A vegetarian diet means you do not eat meat or fish, but still consume milk, cheese, eggs and honey. A vegan diet means you do not consume meat, fish, eggs, milk, butter or any other animal by-product. Because a vegan diet is fairly limited, you need to be very aware of the nutritional content of the foods you do eat in order to maintain a balanced diet.

A vegetarian diet is easy to follow and is an extremely healthy diet option. For instance, an animal-free diet has none of the 'wrong' type of fat we mentioned before. However, you must make sure that you replace meat with alternative sources of protein.

This menu will give you a daily requirement of protein:

Easy peasy. If soup is not to your liking how about baked beans or brown rice with cheese or corn or nuts? Or a veggie chilli followed by yoghurt? Mmmm, think I'll go raid the fridge. Back in a minute.

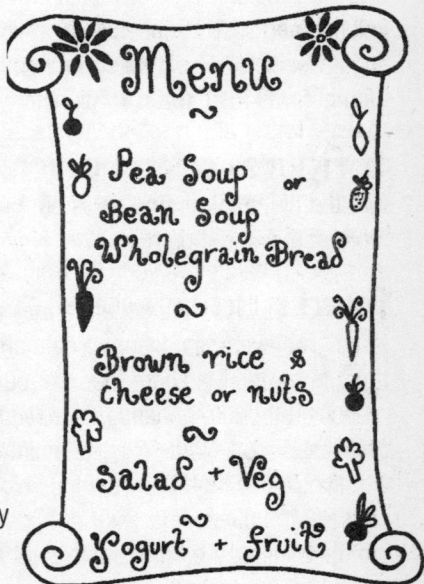

Menu

~

Pea Soup or Bean Soup
Wholegrain Bread

~

Brown rice & cheese or nuts

~

Salad + Veg

~

Yogurt + fruit

read the label

Label-reading is much fun (ahem) when shopping for food. The fact that you may not buy your own food is not an excuse; you'd be doing your whole family a good turn if you trail the supermarket aisles with your parents nagging them into buying healthy stuff. You especially need to check fat, sugar, salt, additives and E-number contents. It's not just biscuits that contain the sweet stuff; it's even added to foods like tomato ketchup and soup to enhance their flavour. Whenever possible, choose sugar-free versions of muesli, orange juice and yoghurt, and go for more natural foods than frozen TV dinners.

If figures aren't given, remember that the higher an ingredient is on the label, the more of it is in the product.

Food additives are a major nutrition issue. The average consumer eats around 2.5kg of them in a year. Many are there for purely cosmetic reasons; others to enhance the flavour of the processed food. Some experts maintain that additives can kill off the vitamins in food and may cause asthma, eczema, migraine, dizziness, stomach pains and other unpleasant symptoms in those who are sensitive to them.

INGREDIENTS
Sugar, Flour,
Preservatives
Emulsifiers
E numbers

Chocolate
Biscuits

Label low-down

🌀 Flavourings: enhance flavour.

★ Colourings: make food look more appealing.

🌀 Preservatives: slow down the rate at which products go off. Some
are included to stop artificial colourings fading and flavourings
deteriorating.

★ Emulsifiers: enable water to be used in a product. Water improves
the texture and increases the products' weight.

🌀 Stabilisers: stop water and fat in food separating, so it always
looks smooth and creamy.

★ Anti-caking agents: stop food from turning lumpy.

🌀 Sweeteners: make foods taste sweeter.

Some food additives are given E-numbers which makes them easy to
identify on the label. Although some – such as E102 (tartrazine) – are
more likely to cause health problems than others, it is best to be on
the safe side and choose foods that have the fewest number of
additives or, preferably, none at all.

This healthy eating lark doesn't mean you can never
eat chocolate again or that all your meals will revolve around bean
sprouts. All you need to do is make sure that most of your diet is
healthy, and that not-so-healthy food is in the minority. You can still
indulge at a burger bar so long as you don't do it every day.

Incidentally the majority of people who have a healthy diet
don't miss junk food. After a period of eating well, most peeps find they
don't like the taste of highly-processed, artificially-coloured and
-flavoured food anymore.

debunking dieting

The most common arguments, knocked well and truly on the head

"I weigh more than I did two years ago."

Weight gain is natural as your body grows. If you happen to put on a few pounds don't automatically blame the cake you ate last week. It's probably more to do with your body developing and changing throughout puberty.

"My clothes don't fit me any more."

During puberty your body will change dimensions, especially around your thighs, bum and bust. This doesn't mean you're getting fat – it does mean you're growing up and that you need to buy some new clothes. Hurrah! an excuse to go shopping.

Excuse to go shopping

"All my friends are on diets."

So whoever did anything just because their mates did? You might feel left out if you're chomping your way through a hearty lunch while they nibble around the edge of a slimming biscuit (though somehow I doubt it), but chances are they're hungrily wishing they could be eating your lunch!

A Hearty Lunch

"I eat more than all my friends."

So what? Everyone's body uses food at a different rate (your metabolic rate) so the amount different people need to stay healthy varies. It's especially important to eat plenty during this growth stage of your life. Just because your appetite is greater than your mates' only proves that your body is using more energy, is still growing and that you have a faster metabolic rate. The difference could also be due to you being an on-the-go sorta person and your mates being couch potatoes.

"I'm quite skinny and I want to stay this way."

If your body shape is predisposed to change then it will change, unless you are daft enough to deprive yourself of food and become seriously ill. On the flip side, if you are naturally skinny you may be depriving yourself of food for no reason at all – many skinny people can eat as much as they like without putting on weight.

"My boyfriend says I'm a greedy pig."

Your boyfriend is reacting to cultural dictums that say women should constantly 'watch their weight' (except they shouldn't). Kindly inform him that eating is as natural a process as breathing, and as you enjoy it you will carry on. Waiter!

New womanly Curves

"The boys in my class tease me about the size of my bust."

It's not you who's at fault, it's them. If you thought us girls had trouble coming to terms with looking like women, you should realise what a problem boys have with it. Suddenly, all those girls who for years never looked that dissimilar to them take on a new, scary appearance. What's more they find it quite attractive but, erm, aren't quite sure what to do about it. So, being boys they go for the easiest, most immature option which is to pick up on the differences and hurl abuse. Believe it or not it makes them feel better. I know it's hard but you just have to try to rise above their silliness, walk tall and be proud of what you are. The poor dears just need to grow up and when of course they do, will swear that they have always liked women with large breasts. Men! How yawnsome they can be.

"I don't want to be womanly – it's embarrassing."

Do you cringe with embarrassment when you realise you've left your bra in the bathroom and your dad's just gone in there? Do you look in the mirror and, although you look like a woman, still don't feel like one? If so it may be tempting to avoid eating in an effort to stop growing up anymore. Our mind doesn't mature at the same rate as our body, but you can't stop the progression of change. Eventually your attitude will catch up to your bod and you'll think being womanly is perfectly fine. In the meantime, try to talk to someone you can trust about how you feel; you're not alone. What you really need is self-confidence and reassurance that you will be able to cope with and love the new you.

"I'd be really happy if I was thinner."

Happiness comes from within and not from possessing a certain set of vital statistics. If you are trying to diet down to a size 6 in the hope that it will make you happy, forget it. Changing your size won't change your life. Because we're surrounded by advertising images of thin, 'successful' women, we assume that body size is critical to our enjoyment of life. It's not. There are as many unhappy thin people as there are happy fatter people. The problem with our culture is that this truth is not promoted. Happiness is about attitude, not body size.

Dr. Jones

* Check with your doctor before dieting

"But I'm fat!"

If you genuinely feel you are overweight and wish to diet, go to your doctor and ask for a controlled weight-loss plan and a target weight, so you can lose just enough without depriving yourself of essential vitamins and minerals. If

57

your doctor says you don't need to lose weight then accept the advice. Don't buy diet foods and calorie books and let them rule your life. Continual dieting slows your metabolic rate which means that you gradually have to eat less and less in order to lose further weight. Without professional help and sound advice it's very difficult to know when enough is enough; the pursuit of a few more pounds is where diet problems begin. There are too many girls who are obsessed with dieting. Don't be the next casualty.

the importance of exercise

While dieting is the wrong thing for most teenagers to do, exercise gets ten out of ten. Working out certainly tones muscles to enhance any figure type, but the benefits of regular exercise do more than just affect your appearance.

Keeping fit is relatively easy in your teens when there are lots of activities going on at school, and when you tend to be more active anyway because of your lifestyle. Face it, when you haven't got a car, walking and biking are your only options. However, to gain maximum benefit from an exercise regime you need to work out for 20 minutes, three times a week.

Exercise: the benefits.

1 It makes you feel brilliant. This is because working out encourages the release of hormones (endorphins) in your brain that fight stress and make you feel oooh, sooo good.

2 It helps you sleep better.

3 It encourages you to eat a healthy diet. People who work out are more likely to eat well and drink lots of water.

4 It makes you more creative. By saying bye-bye to stress, your brain can work at its peak.

5 It tones your body – good news for any body type.

6 Using energy ultimately gives you more energy.

7 It helps those who want to lose weight to burn calories.

8 You get to wear some nifty outfits.

Exercise

WATER!

Nifty outfit →

Makes you feel Brilliant!

eating disorders

Eating disorders are most common among teenage girls. Although both anorexia nervosa and bulimia nervosa are related to dieting, experts feel these illnesses develop out of factors other than just a desire to lose weight.

Many people blame the images of super-slim models we see in magazines for causing eating disorders, but this is far too simple a theory for what are very complicated illnesses. After all, not everyone who goes on a diet or ogles Naomi and Kate develops anorexia or bulimia.

The causes of anorexia or bulimia are complex, and experts believe they are related to: tension at home, pressure to do well at school, or sexual abuse. You may feel that you have no control over your own life, and that your body weight is the only thing you can control. You may want to resist turning from a girl into a woman, especially if you are anxious about the future.

A symptom of anorexia is, basically, a refusal to eat. The victim will have a very distorted view of how she looks; even though she will eventually lose a lot of weight, she'll still consider herself big. Bulimia is a similar condition characterised by excessive bouts of eating, usually in private, followed by self-induced vomiting or the use of laxatives. Both frequent bingeing and vomiting are bad for your health; they irritate your intestines and disrupt your digestive system.

TOO THIN
↓

Warning signs

☺ If you think you're fat but everyone else says you're too thin.

★ If you hide or lie about the fact that you're dieting.

☺ If you make yourself sick after eating.

★ If you pretend you've eaten when you haven't.

☺ If you have lost a lot of weight and your periods have stopped.

★ If you are growing downy hair on your body. Anorexics often grow hair to compensate for the lack of fat which would otherwise insulate their body from the cold.

☺ Extreme weakness and tiredness.

★ If you are abusing laxatives.

Anorexics and bulimics are often very aware of their condition and will lie to avoid discovery and confrontation. Even when a glimmer of self-realisation strikes, they lack the desire and conviction to do anything about it. It is often up to friends and family to put them in touch with someone who can help. Professional counselling and medical help are essential because both illnesses are extremely dangerous and can result in death.

If you think you know

someone with an eating disorder, tell a teacher or someone who can help them straightaway. Your friend may not thank you immediately, in fact you'll be their worst enemy, but in the long run you will have done them a favour and they will be grateful. Just be supportive and hang on in there.

61

chapter 4

How to have beautiful skin

...glow, baby, glow!

Your skin relies on a balanced diet to remain healthy. Not only does glowing skin look good, it plays a crucial role in protecting your body. Computer boffins use the term 'gigo', which means 'garbage in-garbage out'. This can be applied to the relationship between diet and skin: good stuff in-glowing skin out. Vitamins A, C and E are most commonly associated with healthy skin. Don't fall into the trap of targeting one part of your body through your diet; your whole bod needs to be healthy for all its parts to function best.

If you maintain a balanced, nutritious diet, eating your fair share of fruit, veggies, meat, poultry, seafood, beans, pulses and cereals, drink plenty of good (dead cheap) water, and treat your skin with the respect it deserves, your skin will positively glow. Abuse, neglect and misfeed it and, oh no, it's too awful to contemplate.

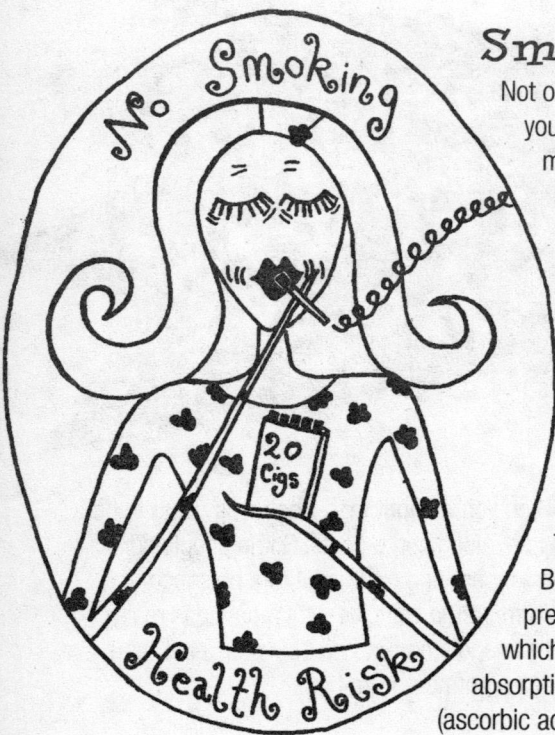

No Smoking
20 Cigs
Health Risk

Smoking

Not only is it incredibly bad for your health, smoking will make you look older, sooner. Looking older doesn't mean that at 14 you'll look like a glamorous 18-year-old if you've got a fag in your mouth. What I mean is that you'll wrinkle sooner, especially around your eyes and mouth. The cause of this is Benzopyrene, a substance present in tobacco smoke, which inhibits your body's absorption of vitamin C (ascorbic acid).

Your body cannot manufacture vitamin C so it relies on you to get it from green leafy vegetables, berries, citrus fruits, asparagus, avocados, broccoli, Brussels sprouts, mangoes, parsley, peas and tomatoes. Eat these regularly and you can forget about supplements. A vitamin C deficiency damages the collagen in your skin's support system, resulting in saggy skin and deep wrinkles. So, as if you didn't know already, don't smoke, okay?

Beauty sleep

It's not just a case of bags under your eyes; if you go without kip you deprive your body of the time it needs to repair cellular damage and renew cells. Average seven to eight hours sleep a night, or suffer the grumpy-skin consequences.

what's that on the end of my nose?

ust when you thought teen-hood was going to be a doddle, along come spots. Some people never get spots, others find them a bit of a nuisance — one or two a month to coincide with a period is really common. But some bods have spots non-stop for several years, and to them puberty seems like a nightmare from hell.

The very last thing you want to hear about spots is: 'You'll grow out of them.' Life is too short to spend it waiting for your spots to take a hike. What you want to hear is how to get rid of them, pronto.

It is possible to get rid of spots, no matter how severe they are. The trouble is most people don't know where to start when it comes to seeing them off. There are so many myths and so many 'on-the-spot'

64

experts, it can be very hard, expensive and time-consuming to tell fact from sales pitch.

Here we are going to reveal the truth about spots – what they are, why they occur, and the best ways to get rid of them. And there's more good news: you don't have to stop eating chocolate. Like I said before – life is just too short.

Spots, zits and acne

A lot of people think that acne is the name for a bad case of spots, but that's not strictly true. Acne is the name of the condition, and spots are the symptoms. If you suddenly get a spot on your nose, previously having none, don't go into a mad panic, the stress will do you no good at all. This rogue spot does not mean acne is coming your way. Oh, and before I forget, zit is just a user-friendly term for spot.

What doesn't cause spots?

You'll be overwhelmed with joy to hear that the formation of spots is way too complicated to be affected by a couple of squares of chocolate. Spots are not caused by eating too much chocolate and junk food (though they certainly don't help your overall health profile), not washing often enough or masturbating. Spots are not passed on when kissing; they are not infectious.

What does cause spots?

The exact cause of acne isn't fully understood, but the factors which contribute to its development are known.

Acne develops in the sebaceous follicles of your skin. These follicles are concentrated on your face, but are also found on your chest and back. Each sebaceous follicle contains a small hair, and a large sebaceous gland, which opens onto the skin via a pore. During puberty (yes, that again), new hormonal activity causes the sebaceous glands to get bigger. Naturally-occurring bacteria from your skin acts upon the sebum (an oily substance which protects skin), produced by the glands, to form fatty acids. The dead skin cells lining the follicle multiply and form a plug. The fatty acids then act upon this plug to form a spot. In short, acne occurs as a result of frenetic, internal, hormonal activity.

Acne can be aggravated by oily suncreams (moderate exposure to sunlight can help clear the condition), some prescribed drugs, working in greasy environments, stress and, of course, periods.

There are several types of spot

Blackheads .... Whiteheads ... Popules .... Cysts ....

66

Blackheads are tiny spots with open tops. The reason they look black isn't because they are full of dirt (they aren't); the discolouration is caused by a natural process within your skin. They crop up on the oiliest areas of your face; usually your nose and chin.

Whiteheads are small, white spots with closed tops. Leave them alone and they will eventually burst.

Papules and pustules are formed when pus collects around a spot, causing breaks in the follicle wall. The inflammation spreads beneath your skin creating larger, raised, red or yellow spots. Again, they usually burst of their own accord.

Nodules or cysts are very inflamed spots lying deep beneath the surface of the skin, so don't even think about bursting them. You will be wasting your time and damaging your skin. Eventually, these large red bumps will be broken down internally.

Squeezing – don't do it!

Squeezing will not get rid of spots. Don't be tempted to squeeze the glaring, bright yellow spot on the end of your nose. And even though you may believe that a secret blackhead squeezing session can do no harm, it will, so don't indulge.

No matter how gently you pop a spot, it is very traumatic on the skin and you risk damaging the follicle beneath the surface, which lets the spot spread further. Yeuch. If you have a fit-to-burst spot, break the surface by ever-so-gently rubbing it with a clean tissue, and then carefully dabbing the debris (a polite name for the gunge that comes out of a spot) away with another clean tissue. Follow-up with a good cleansing session.

how to get rid of spots

f spots are making your life a misery, it's really important to get proper treatment. Acne can affect your self-esteem, especially in severe cases which can last for years and cause scarring.

Try skin care products which contain special anti-spot ingredients like Salicylic acid 2% which can help unblock pores; or Benzoyl peroxide. This is an anti-bacterial agent which is absorbed into the skin and acts upon the naturally-occurring but harmful bacteria in the follicle. Follow the instructions very carefully, you'll need to use it for a few weeks to see any results. Benzoyl peroxide creams are available in various strengths – from 2.5 per cent to 10 per cent – and it is always a good idea to try the weakest concentration first.

If this doesn't work then go to your doctor who will be able to prescribe various remedies including antibiotic treatments to be taken internally or applied directly to the skin. Although you may not see instant results – many take up to six months to do their stuff – they are extremely successful in clearing or controlling even severe cases of spots. If the first treatment doesn't work, go back for another formulation. A doctor may recommend a combination of Tretinoin lotion or gel and antibiotic cream for mild acne, or in more severe cases antibiotic tablets or capsules.

A doctor may refer you to a dermatologist for specialist treatment. Do not worry – spots can be beaten!

Other avenues of treatment are plant extracts, herbal poultices (a nasty-sounding name for a thick, mask-like cream), face washes, and even herbal teas. Herbalists recommend drinking lots of water, avoiding fried and over-processed foods, sun and smoking (no surprise there, eh!). It could even be that your skin condition is in part due to an allergy. For advice on alternative treatments, like herbalism and homeopathy, go to a reputable practitioner or a specialist health shop. Even your local chemist may have some imaginative suggestions. The down side to this approach is that, unlike conventional medicine, you cannot currently get treatment through the National Health Service, which means you might have to fork out a lot of money, over a long period of time.

Herbalism herbs

know your skin type

Your skin type is governed by how much sebum your skin produces. Sebum is necessary because it makes your skin soft and supple. This elasticity is the skin's effective means of self protection.

Normal skin produces just enough sebum to keep it looking and feeling perfectly gorgeous. Least likely major moan: 'Oooh I hate my skin.'

Oily skin is the most common among teen-types. The skin produces too much sebum which creates an oily sheen on the face. This is actually not all oil – it's a mix of sebum and sweat. How lovely. Oily skin is more prone to spots. Most-likely major moan: 'Oooh, I hate my greasy skin and the spots that come with it.'

Dry skin looks rough and flaky, and feels taut. This is because the skin doesn't let go of its dead skin cells quickly enough, so they hang around looking dull and dry like autumn leaves which refuse to fall. Dry skin is linked to a lack of sebum production. Most likely major moan: 'Oooh, why have I got skin like sandpaper?'

70

Combination skin means that part of your face, usually referred to as the 'T-zone' and including your forehead, nose and chin, is oily; the rest is normal or dry. This occurs because you have more sebaceous glands in the T-zone than in other areas. Most likely major moan: 'My nose is spotty but the rest of my face is fine.'

Whatever your skin type there are skin care products – over-the-counter or home-brew – to suit you. However, no amount of bathroom-shelf fillers will compensate for regular washing, a good diet, sound sleep, relaxation and exercise.

Skin kit

Facial skin care products like cleansers, toners, moisturisers, masks and scrubs all claim to improve your skin. But let's get one thing straight from the start. The combination of mild, unperfumed or moisturising soap and warm water makes an extremely effective cleanser, and if you're satisfied with this method, then carry on. You don't necessarily need anything else.

For those who wish to crowd the bathroom shelf with important-looking lotions and potions, or if you just enjoy the process of cleansing and caring for your skin, here's a guide to the basic kit:

Cleansers
Non-soap cleansers such as creams, lotions, or rinse-off gels tend to have a less drying-out effect on the skin than soap. Cream cleansers are best at removing make-up, and are designed to be wiped off with tissue or cotton wool. Rinse-off cleansers are quicker to use because you simply wash them off with lukewarm water. Both are just as effective at cleansing as soap, but can cost more.

There are cleansers aplenty on shop shelves, or you can whip one up at home. One popular straight-from-the-fridge face cleaner is tomato. (You're not allergic are you?) Mash the tomato to a pulp and leave it on your face for 10-15 minutes and remove with warm water. Only a couple of words of advice: don't answer the door or start chatting up the salad dressing. Cleopatra used to bathe in a milk bath, and pundits have it that a little milk on cotton wool rubbed gently over the face is a terrific cleanser for delicate skin.

Toners
These remove traces of cleanser left behind on your skin. Some skin care experts claim that they're also good for removing soap residue.

It's best to choose a mild toner or skin freshener, rather than harsh astringent toners which contain a higher concentration of alcohol. These products often claim to remove excess oil and tighten pores but their effectiveness is debatable. Some experts claim that by removing too much oil from the skin your complexion reacts by churning out even more oil to replace it. Also, the pore closing action is only temporary. If

Toning
Cold
Water
Splash face

you don't think a toner is your line of country, splash your face with cold water after cleansing. It can help circulation, temporarily close the pores, and wake you up. Mashed cucumber also makes a good toner astringent. Believe me, it works.

Moisturisers
These stop your skin from losing moisture content more quickly than it can replace it. Moisturisers make your skin feel soft and supple.

Most teenagers don't really need much – or sometimes any – moisturiser. Choose one which is very light to avoid putting too much oil onto your skin which could aggravate spots.

Wear moisturiser if...

☺ Your skin tends to be dry or feels 'tight' after cleansing.

★ You like to wear foundation. A moisturiser helps it sit smoothly on your skin.

★**Hint** In cold weather the temperature isn't the only skin-drying culprit; central heating can dry out the atmosphere leaving your skin desperate for some moisturising protection. A simple strategy to lessen the effect of central heating is to place a bowl of water next to you when you sleep.

Facial scrubs

Skin is in a constant state of change, and dead skin cells are pushed to the surface where they drop or are washed off. Facial scrubs remove these cells as they build up, so that fresher-looking skin beneath can show through. Because of the rate at which skin sheds its dead cells you only need to use a facial scrub every week or so. Use gentle, circular movements, avoiding the delicate skin around your eyes and lips.

Face masks

Clay-based face masks clean the skin by drawing out the impurities. You apply them wet, and once in contact with the air they dry and tighten, trapping the dirt, oil and dead skin cells that the clay has drawn from the skin. When you rinse off the mask, the gunge goes with it. Some masks claim to close pores, but as with toning products the effect is temporary. Use a mask once a fortnight; more often and you could irritate your skin.

Draws out impurities

CLAY MASK

Gorgeousness guidelines

Cleanse your face twice a day, morning and evening.

If you have oily or combination skin, choose a moisturiser and foundation that are water-based and oil-free. If a product is labelled 'non-comedogenic', it won't aggravate spots.

74

🌀 Don't feel you have to spend lots of money on toiletries for oily, spotty skin which claim to remove surface oil and grime. They have a limited value because – repeat after me – spots are formed by internal hormonal activity, and cosmetics and toiletries are not allowed by law to interfere with hormonal activity. However, products for oily skin do have some benefits: they can make your skin look fresher, feel cleaner and reduce the shine that characterises spotty skin.

⭐ Whatever your skin type be gentle when following your beauty regime. Your skin will suffer if you are rough.

🌀 Some people have sensitive skin, and certain ingredients in cosmetics cause their skin to feel tight and itchy, to flake or develop a rash. Two of the most common irritants are fragrance and colour, and as neither has any effect on how well a skin care product works, it's best to use non-perfumed products to which artificial colouring has not been added. Hypoallergenic products, which are widely available, are formulated for sensitive skin and contain only the most necessary ingredients.

⭐ No one needs to put moisturiser on their nose, unless it's sunburnt. Tut tut.

🌀 If you have severe acne don't use masks or scrubs, as they may aggravate your spots. Your doctor will be able to advise you on the best skin care regime for your complexion.

GENTLE
LOTION
no fragrance
no colour
no Aggravation
Hypo - Allergenic

No Animal Testing

Kind to you, kind to animals?

Many people choose a brand of cosmetics because the label says they have not been tested on animals. In fact, nearly all ingredients will have been tested on animals at some point because of mandatory safety requirements.

Cosmetics companies

which make a 'not tested on animals' claim will often only use ingredients which were animal-tested before a certain date. Because of this self-imposed restriction they will not use newly-tested ingredients and their product range may be limited. They argue, however, that there are more than enough effective, and tested, ingredients around already.

Other companies which are 'against animal testing' choose to use a five-year rolling system. This means they will not use ingredients that have been tested on animals within the last five years, but once this period has passed they will take them up. They claim that this encourages manufacturers to seek alternative methods of testing.

In some cases, a cosmetics company will say that they do not test on animals, or claim that the finished product isn't tested. However, they may have paid someone else to test it, or the products' ingredients may have been tested on animals. The only way to be sure is to write to the company and ask for their policy on animal testing.

Those cosmetics companies which continue to test ingredients on animals do so because they wish to develop new ingredients, and the current law gives them no alternative.

skin & the sun

You may think that a deep, golden tan is the most attractive thing on the planet. You may love lying in the sun, soaking up the rays. You might even secretly relish picking at peeling, sunburnt skin. Having the most noticeable tan lines may make you feel like the most envied girl in your class, and your brown legs may make your new white skirt look really hot. You may just believe a golden tan makes you look healthy. How wrong can you be. It is time we all accepted that sunbathing is a thing of the past.

Tanned and especially burnt skin is skin that has been damaged. When exposed to strong sunlight, your skin turns brown to protect itself. Unfortunately, many people have skin that is simply too fair to tan quickly enough, so they burn.

Even when the tan or the burn fades,

the damage done is irreparable. In fact, it gradually builds up over the years of exposure to sunlight and causes your skin to age. This is why your mum's skin looks older than yours, and your gran's looks even older. At the moment 'looking old' is the least of your problems, but you will probably feel very different about it in a few years time.

Even more serious is that sun-damaged skin is at risk of developing skin cancer, and although it is curable if treated early it still has very serious implications for your health.

Repeated bad sunburns are thought to greatly increase your chances of developing skin cancer. At present, skin cancer is increasing by about ten per cent each year.

That's why dermatologists recommend that you don't sunbathe, that you wear sunscreen on any exposed skin and to slap on a hat whenever you are out in the sun.

You need to use a sun cream with a high SPF (sun protection factor) number – make sure it is SPF 8 or higher – to stop the sun's rays from being absorbed by your skin.

SPF numbers

These are a measure of the protection against the burning UVB rays that a suncream gives to your skin. The greater the SPF number, the greater the protection. SPF 25 is a total sun block, affording the highest level of protection so far available. Dermatologists advise that no one should wear less than an SPF8 in sunny weather. All but the highest factors allow you to tan.

Low number SPF creams allow you to tan slightly, but you shouldn't wear them until your skin has slowly acclimatised to the sun. Wear a high number SPF for the first couple of days into a holiday. As even the smallest amount of tanning will damage your skin, it's best to forget about sunbathing altogether.

If you have a darker olive or Afro-Caribbean skin colour you don't have to worry too much about burning; but you're still at risk. If you visit a country with a much hotter climate than ours, for instance, you may find that your skin can't adjust quickly enough, so it's wise to use sun protection creams with a mid-range SPF.

The star system

This is an indication of the protection that a sunscreen gives against ageing UVA rays. A rating of four stars is best. A tan only protects your skin against UVB rays, so even though you may switch to a lower SPF rating sun cream, you should still continue to use a product that gives four-star UVA protection.

Brownie guide

🌀 If you are out in the sun reapply suncream every two hours and wear a waterproof cream when swimming.

⭐ Sunscreen isn't just for holidays – you need to use it in this country too. Even on cloudy days harmful rays can still penetrate the clouds.

🌀 Don't forget to apply suncream lavishly to vulnerable areas like the tops of your feet, shoulders, nose and ears.

⭐ A sun hat with a wide brim will give additional protection, as will heavy-weave white clothes.

🌀 Avoid strong sunlight between 11am and 3pm when the sun is at its strongest.

⭐ Never apply oil to your skin in an attempt to tan quickly; it is a sure fire way of getting a nasty burn. Think of chips sizzling away in a frying pan – enough said?

🌀 Your lips have no natural sun protection system, so to prevent them burning you must wear a special, total-block lip balm.

★ Don't use sun beds: the rays they use are thought to be harmful to your skin, and may suppress your immune system.

🌀 Wear good sunglasses, not on your head, but on your eyes. Not only does the sun damage your eyes, but all that squinting can give you the most awful lines. Look for the British Standard kite mark bearing BS2724 for an assurance that the glasses will protect your eyes from solar radiation and the rest, and guarantee minimum distortion and lens strength. Imported sunglasses may use the BS equivalent of CE89686. Glasses labelled UV400 indicates good UV protection. Once you've donned your sunnies, pose away to your heart's content.

What to do if you burn

You can't reverse the long-term damage, but you can make yourself feel more comfortable and minimise peeling.

★ Cover up, apply sunblock to any skin still exposed and get out of the sun as quickly as possible.

🌀 Drink lots of water to stop dehydration.

★ Take a cool shower to lower the temperature of your skin.

🌀 Apply after-sun treatment cream to moisturise your skin. Some

81

people believe that vitamin E cream can be a great help. In Australia, they apply cold plain yoghurt to the burnt area, leave it a couple of minutes and then rinse off with warm water. Slices of cucumber gently rubbed on the skin can also temporarily ease the pain.

★ Stay out of the sun until your skin has healed completely.

UV protection make-up

You can buy moisturisers, foundations and make-up which contain UV protection, but unless the packaging gives a high SPF number don't rely on them to protect your skin. Without an SPF number, you have no idea of the level of protection on offer.

fake it!

So, no more suntan, huh? Hang on, all this doesn't mean you can't look tanned. Fake tanners are not only completely safe, they can also give you a very realistic looking tan in a matter of hours. Fake tanners have also come of age. Gone are those smelly potions of a few years ago which turned your skin fluorescent orange. Today's products are pleasing to use, and give you a natural colour.

Fake tans work by dyeing brown the very fine top layer of skin. It takes a few hours for the colour to develop, and it lasts for around three days. After three days that top layer of skin naturally flakes away in minute specks, taking your fake tan with it. Always test a new tanning product on a small patch of skin, to see how the colour develops on your skin type and to make sure the tanner doesn't cause any irritation. Tanners are waterproof, and once developed won't stain your clothes. Some tanners contain moisturisers and low SPF sun filters while others are specially made for facial bronzing.

Getting the best results

1 Start by exfoliating your skin to remove dead skin cells, paying extra attention to dry areas like elbows, back of heels and knees. This not only helps your tan go on more evenly, it also helps it last longer. Apply moisturiser to your body about half an hour before slapping on the tanner. Smear petroleum jelly onto your eyebrows and hairline to stop the tanner collecting in the hairs and giving you darker areas.

2 Take care applying the tanning lotion to ankles, elbows, knees, neck and the backs of heels, as these areas 'absorb' tanners more easily than the rest of your body.

3 Cream which isn't absorbed into your skin can stain clothes, so it's

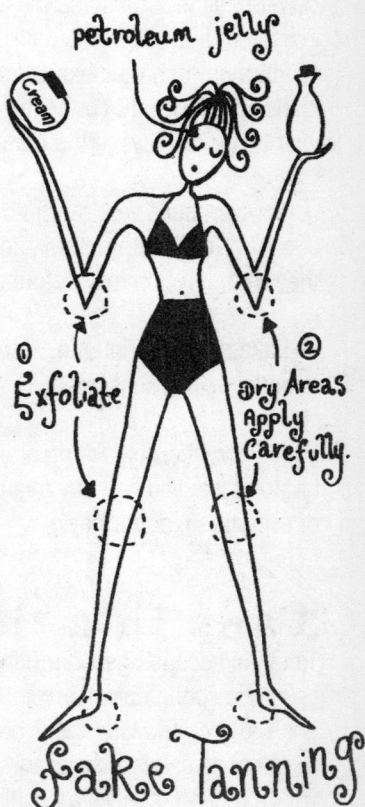

petroleum jelly

Cream

① Exfoliate

② Dry Areas Apply Carefully.

fake Tanning

best to wear an old dressing gown until it has been absorbed.

Wear an old Dressing gown.

Step 3

4 Apply the cream liberally to all areas you want to tan. If you apply enough cream it won't streak, so don't skimp.

5 Only apply fake tan to areas that would normally turn brown in the sun. So don't put it on the palms of your hands or the soles of your feet, and go easy between your fingers and toes.

6 Always wash your hands immediately after applying a fake tan. Dark brown palms are a dead giveaway that you spent your holidays in the bathroom, not in the Bahamas.

7 You can build your tan gradually by applying more tanner every day or so. Sounds sorta natural, doesn't it? Allow three to five hours for the tan to develop fully before giving yourself a second coat.

8 Fake tan does not offer a sufficient level of sun protection; you still need to wear a sunscreen.

If it all goes horribly wrong or your hands look like you've been digging up potatoes, you can buy a fake tan fading lotion. Some peeps think of everything, don't they?

Tans in a tick

To tan in seconds get your hands on a bottle of skin tint. Apply with a cosmetic sponge all over your body. You'll have a tan in seconds, but don't expect it to last: these products aren't waterproof. Bronzing powders give your face a tan-like glow. Apply with a blusher brush to your forehead, cheeks and chin. Be sparing or you'll look like you tripped up in a tin of gravy browning.

teeth

Going to the dentist may not be the coolest thing on the planet, but then, neither are dentures. As you get older and take more responsibility for yourself, looking after your teeth might just fall by the wayside as one of those 'I can't be bothered' issues. However, if you don't take care of 'em, they may not be around for as long as you are. Preventative dental care is really important, even more so if you wear braces where getting into all the nooks and crannies is just that much harder.

Visit your dentist every six months

for a check-up (usually free for under-16s).
If you are terrified of going, tell them; the best surgeries have all sorts of effective techniques to help you relax.

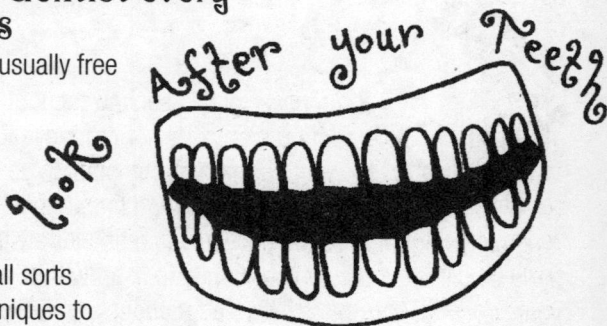

look After your Teez?

Have your teeth cleaned by a dental hygienist every three months. They will also show you how to clean your teeth properly. And if you want to give yourself a fright, ask for a disclosing tablet. Disclosing tablets reveal just how much gunge (plaque) is left on your teeth after inadequate brushing. Yuk!

Clean your teeth twice a day, more if you like, as the hygienist has shown you. Cleaning your teeth also freshens your mouth and your breath in readiness for some close-quarter talking.

Floss your teeth every night. Not so much to ask, is it?

nails

You never give a second thought to your nails until puberty. It's not that anything special happens to them at this point in your life – just that you suddenly get the urge to dab lurid-coloured polish on them. Next thing you know you've set to work with a nail file, and hey, all of a sudden your hands look grown up. How you care for your nails and your hands says a lot about you. So go on, pamper yourself a little.

How to do a home manicure

1 Remove any old nail polish with nail polish remover.

2 Soak your fingertips in a bowl of warm, soapy water for five minutes to soften your skin and nails, then dry.

3 Apply cuticle cream to the base and sides of your nails. This softens the skin that overlaps each nail.

4 File your nails using the smoother side of an emery board, moving in one direction only. A slightly-rounded nail extending just beyond the fingertip is the strongest and most modern style – talons are out.

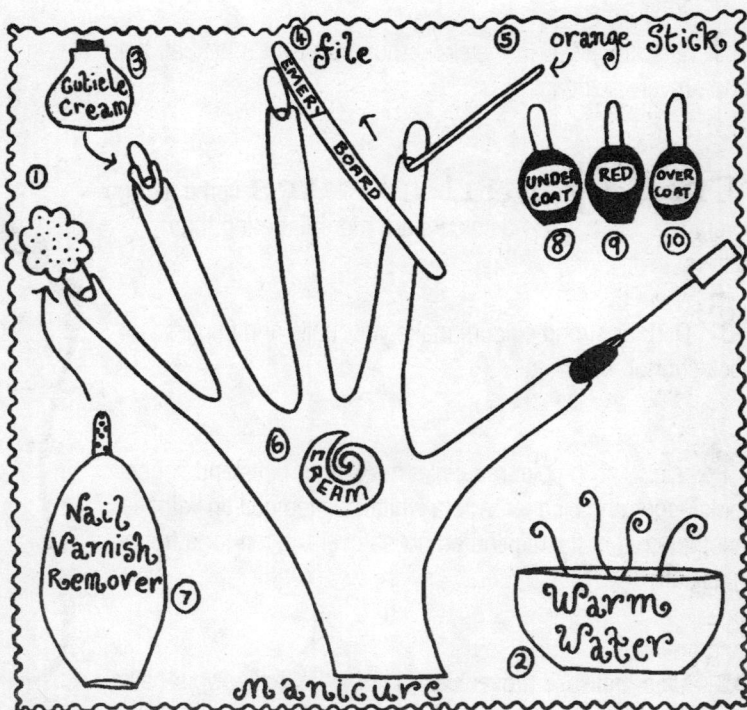

manicure

5 Use an orange stick wrapped in cotton wool to gently push the cuticles back.

6 Rub in a big dollop of hand cream.

7 Wipe your nails over with nail polish remover to remove any grease.

8 Apply a coat of undercoat. This clear polish stops stronger coloured polishes from staining the nail.

9 Add your chosen nail colour, allow to dry for ten minutes and then add a second coat.

10 Finish with a protective top coat to stop the polish chipping.

11 Rub almond oil in the skin around your nails to keep them strong and prevent splitting.

Trendy nail colours come and go

every season, but some colours are more flattering than others.

Dark or strong colours make your nails and fingers look shorter.

★ Light, flesh coloured pinks make your nails and fingers look longer and cleaner. Add a white-painted nail tip with another coat of flesh coloured polish over the top for a french manicure.

Clear polish is most wearable of all. It makes your nails look shiny and healthy.

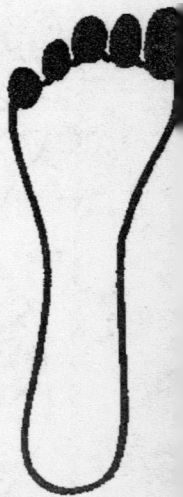

best foot forward

kay, so no-one can see your feet for DMs and stacked boots, but that doesn't mean you can ignore your tootsies. Hardworking feet deserve a little tenderness so, go on, indulge them in a pedicure.

1 Soak your feet in warm water to soften the skin. Mix a cup of bicarbonate of soda into two to three litres of warm water for a wonderfully soothing foot bath.

2 Gently exfoliate dry, rough or hard skin using a pumice stone.

3 Massage in some foot lotion. Those which contain peppermint are very cooling and soothing. If you've no special foot lotion to hand, a good intensive body moisturiser will do.

4 File or cut toe nails straight across so that they are just shorter than the ends of your toes.

5 Use foam toe separators, or cotton wool, to stop your polish smudging.

6 Apply one broad stroke of polish (or a dab on smaller nails) to the centre of each nail.

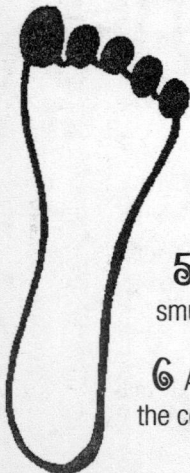

chapter 5

No more bad hair days

...here's to crowning glories

It's really easy to get your hair to look good. However, it is also easy to end up looking like you've been dragged through a hedge backwards. The trick is to understand your hair type, know which techniques and products will work for you, and then practise until you are a hairdressing genius.

The great thing about hair is that whatever you do, it will grow back, so make the most of the follicle fun that's to be had!

Know your hair type

Understanding your hair type allows you to know exactly what looks you are going to be able to achieve with it. I am glad to say that finding this out doesn't mean setting up a complicated scientific experiment in the bathroom. Nor does it depend upon a drawn-out mathematical equation involving the diameter of each hair, multiplied by its length and then divided by how often you wash it. No sirree. To become fully acquainted with your hair type just look in the mirror.

What colour is it?

No, I'm not insulting your intelligence; hair colour does matter. You see, hair that is naturally very dark out-shines fair hair. The colour of your locks will also tell you, without counting on your fingers, approximately how many hairs you have: blondes average about 120,000 hairs, brunettes around 100,000 and redheads just 80,000. Hair colour is also a ready-reckoner for hair thickness: blonde hairs are usually quite thin or fine, darker hairs are thicker, while red hair is quite often thick and coarse.

What texture is it?

Dead straight hair shines much more than curly hair because the surface of each hair is smooth, and reflects light easily.

Curly hairs have an uneven surface (you could only see this under a strong microscope) that don't reflect light well. The curlier your hair the more obvious this is, which is why some people's crowning glory looks dull no matter how well they look after it.

The most common hair type is somewhere between the two – more or less wavy. Wavy hair is the easiest to style because of its versatility. You can encourage the curl or straighten it, so long as you know and use the proper techniques.

No one hair texture, colour or length is 'better' than any other; the skill in making the most of your hair is to enhance what you've got. Don't try to force it into a style, it's bound not to suit you.

looking after your hair

ow you look after your hair will determine how it looks. The three most important things you can do for your hair after (you guessed it) eating well, sleeping well and getting lots of fresh air, are cleansing, conditioning and having it cut professionally. Don't expect a miracle from a bottle of shampoo if you skip breakfast, smoke, and exist on a diet of chocolate and doughnuts.

The most often asked hair care questions

"How often should I wash my hair?"
If you don't wash your hair often enough your scalp will be itchy, and your hair will look dull and greasy. Some people find that they can go

for days and days without washing it, others have to lather up religiously every two days.

Ideally, you should wash your hair just before it reaches the dull, itchy and greasy stage; about two or three times a week.

You may feel that your hair needs washing more often if you have exercised, are working in a smoky or greasy environment, spend heaps of time in heavy smog areas, or in hot weather when you sweat more. It will also need more frequent washing if you use lots of styling products.

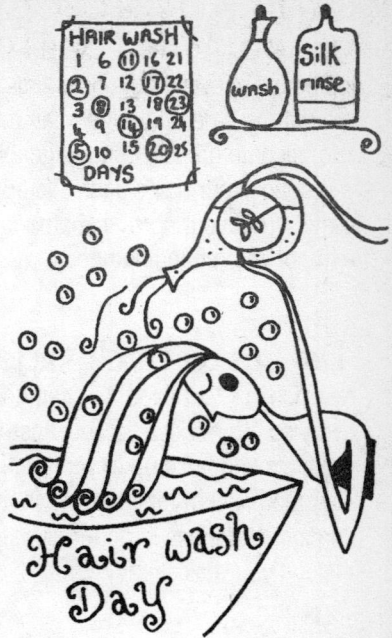

Hair wash Day

"Is it possible to wash hair too often?"

Yes. If your hair isn't dirty, there is no benefit in washing it. Hair that is over-washed tends to be flyaway and fluffy because you may have stripped it of natural oils. It is also harder to style; a little natural oil helps hair to hold a style.

"Which shampoo should I use?"

There are zillions of shampoos on the market, and no, they're not all the same. Choose a shampoo that complements your hair – greasy, dry, normal, dandruff, permed or coloured is the usual choice. If you wash your hair every day get a frequent-wash formulation. There are special shampoos to use after swimming in chlorinated water.

"My hair goes berserk just before my period. What can I do?"

Increased activity in the oil glands of the scalp during puberty and around the time of a period can make your hair behave strangely. It can become greasy, unmanageably wild or as flat as a pancake. When you notice your hair's alter-ego appearing, it might be an idea to switch from your normal shampoo and conditioner to ones formulated to meet your changing needs.

"Do I need to change shampoo regularly?"

Hair doesn't 'get used' to shampoo, so there's no need to change every so often. However, because some conditioners and styling products can build up in your hair, it's worth using a deep-cleansing shampoo once a month to wash away residue. You may also need to change shampoos in hotter climates when your scalp sweats more, making your hair greasy.

"How can I treat dandruff?"

Problem dandruff is thought to be caused by a fungal infection and accelerated hormonal reactions which causes new skin cells to be pushed out of your scalp before the old ones are ready to go. The result is an itchy scalp and loose, white flakes of skin. It can be treated with medicated shampoos from your chemist.

Everyone suffers from dandruff to some extent . You may have a naturally dry scalp, or inadequate rinsing after washing your hair may cause left-over detergents to dry out your scalp. Many suspect that dandruff is stress-related. So if you start flaking all over your exam papers when you've never flaked before, that could be your answer.

As well as medicated shampoos, you can also try various scalp treatments and dandruff shampoos formulated to loosen dead skin cells

94

and moisturise your scalp. Herbalists recommend a hair rinse of rosemary or thyme to stem dandruff. To make a hair rinse, boil the herb (about half a cup) in half a litre of water, cool then strain, reserving the liquid. Next time you shampoo, rinse with your herbal concoction.

"Why do I need conditioner?"

While shampoos cleanse your hair, conditioners make it shiny and manageable by smoothing and lightly coating the surface of each hair. Conditioners are most effective on long hair that tangles easily, and tends to be split and brittle at the ends. You should never comb long, wet hair unless it has a conditioner on it. Hair that is coloured, permed or dry also looks and feels better after conditioning.

Short hair that is already shiny and manageable may not need conditioning. In fact, using it may make your hair so smooth and shiny that you won't be able to do a thing with it.

"What type of conditioner is best?"

You need a conditioner which suits your hair type. If you use one that is too light its conditioning properties won't be sufficient to make a difference to your hair. One that's too heavy may make your hair lank, greasy and impossible to style.

Generally speaking, all-in-one shampoos and conditioners offer the lightest conditioning treatment, followed by rinse-out conditioners. Leave-in conditioners tend to be a little heavier. Intensive treatments,

such as hot wax conditioners and treatment waxes, which are left on your hair for a period of time before being rinsed out, have the deepest conditioning properties.

"How often should I condition my hair?"

Every time you shampoo it. Wet hair is very vulnerable to damage because it loses elasticity, and a conditioner will help protect it by making it less likely to tangle and easier to comb. The benefits of most conditioners only last from one shampoo to the next, so if you miss out on conditioning it will show in the look, feel and manageability of your hair straight away.

"Do conditioning needs change?"

You need to switch to a more intensive conditioner if you have your hair permed, relaxed or coloured. A holiday in the sun, where you spend lots of time in the water, may require a change from a light conditioner to a heavier one. Don't forget to change your shampoo as well.

"Are shampoos and conditioners made with fruit any good?"

Both shampoos and conditioners often contain ingredients which you might not immediately associate with hair care: fruit, nuts and flowers, for instance. Sometimes the manufacturer simply adds a synthetic fragrance and colouring to make the product look and smell appealing but with no real

Wonder fruit

BANANA

Shampoo

benefit for your hair. Others use the real ingredients as part of the products' cleansing or conditioning properties. While they do work, they cost more than basic ranges which are often just as efficient, if not quite so attractive. If you want to indulge, go ahead. But don't feel that you're committing a terrible hair crime if you leave them on the chemists' shelf.

"How often should I get my hair cut?"

Hair grows around 1/4 of an inch (6mm) a month, so to keep short hair looking stylish, and to avoid the 'growing out' look, it needs to be cut every six weeks.

To keep long hair looking really good it should be trimmed every two months, even if you are trying to grow it. This is because the end tips of your hair are most prone to damage, like split-ends, which cannot be repaired. A timely snip is the only way to keep it in check. And while we are talking about split-ends, don't spend your time during deadly-dull lessons hunting down and splitting split-ends further. You're not doing your hair any favours, and it makes you cross-eyed in the process. Always apply extra conditioner to hair ends.

"Can I trim my own hair?"

Not unless you want a ski-slope fringe and a wonky length. Even hairdressers don't cut their own hair, so what hope do you have with a pair of dressmaking shears in front of your bedroom mirror? Follicle carnage can only result.

Hair, sun and chlorine

Just like your skin, your hair suffers under the sun. Strong sunlight causes it to dry out. Fair hair is more vulnerable than dark hair because it contains less protective pigment, and straight hair more than curly because of the angle at which the light hits each hair. You are also more likely to suffer if your hair has undergone a weakening chemical process, such as perming or colouring.

The best way to protect your hair is to pile it up under a sun hat. You can also invest in products which contain UV filters. Unfortunately, there is no SPF system for hair products, so if in doubt about the level of protection on offer, grab a hat.

If you regularly swim in chlorinated water, you should wash your hair immediately on leaving the pool. Chlorine dries hair, and if left unchecked will give fair hair a greenish tint. Anti-chlorine shampoos remove the oxidised metals that cause discolouration and will dispel the distinctive chlorine smell.

pain-free hair cuts

airdressers do a whole lot more than trim hair. A new hairdo can transform you from schoolgirl to siren, and give your hair body, texture and shape that you never thought possible. It can also emphasise good facial features, and play down those you're not so keen on. But don't use a forehead-covering fringe to hide spots. The oil in your hair will only exacerbate the problem. Following are the six steps to styling success.

1 Raid your stack of magazines and cut out pictures of hair styles you like.

2 Eliminate those which you know won't suit your hair, lifestyle or budget. For example, having a perm before going on a sun, surf and sand holiday may not be the best hair care solution. If you're always late for everything, a style that requires lots of time-consuming fiddling is most probably not for you. If you play lots of sport, locks which can't be tied back or pinned up may cause you more grief than they're worth.

3 Take all your hair-style finalists along with you to the hairdressers. You might even like to get some valued second opinions from family and mates, especially if you plan a radical change.

4 When you make an appointment you will be asked if you want a wet or dry cut. For the pure luxury of having someone else shampoo, condition and massage your hair, spend the extra pound or two – it's well worth it and makes the stylist's job easier. But if pennies or time are tight, or if the cut is only a minor one – go for a dry cut.

5 When you get to the hairdresser's your stylist will ask you how you want your hair to look, so now's your chance to say. Don't be backward in coming forward – spread out your gallery of pictures and be prepared to take advice. He or she will know that certain cuts will not do justice to your hair type or face shape. A stylist is there to make you look great. Remember, you're a walking-talking advertisement for their business.

6 While your hairdresser is cutting your hair, get all the info on how to look after and style your new look. Using the right styling tools at home is as important as it is in the hairdresser's, so get as much advice as you can.

home styling

f you thought the choice of shampoos and conditioners overwhelming, then prepare to be totally confounded by the range of styling products. There are so many different types available, it's very easy to pick the wrong one and end up sporting a low-growing shrub, when all you wanted was a sleek, shiny barnet. So, to make life a tad easier, here's a guide to what's what.

Gel
Sticky stuff that can be used on wet hair to encourage it to hold a style. It works best on short, wet hair when you want lots of texture and body, or on short, dry hair to create a slicked look.

Mousse
A light styling product which gives your hair body, and helps it to hold a style. You only use it on wet hair and it's suitable for any length.

Serums
These are a cross between a styling product and a conditioner. You use them on long, wet hair to encourage extra body and shine.

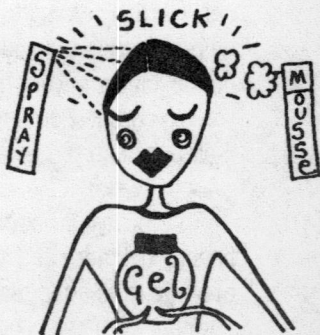

Wax The heaviest styling formulation of them all. Use just a tiny bit on short, dry hair to get lots of texture, hold and shine.

Hairspray Designed to hold your finished look in place. Be mindful of CFCs (which destroy the ozone layer) and buy non-aerosol, pump-action hairsprays. Before commercial hairsprays were available, they were made, at home, using lemons. You don't believe me? Well, unbelievers take heed: lemons contain pectin which is used to help jams set and it can do the same for your hair. Chop two lemons into half a litre of water and simmer on the stove until the lemons are soft. Cool and strain. Put the liquid into a pump-action bottle and refrigerate until needed. If the lacquer is too sticky, add extra water.

Thermal sprays These products don't actually style your hair, but protect it from the heat of hot stylers.

Shine enhancers Available in serums or sprays, you apply them to styled, dry hair to give it a very noticeable gloss. The effect is temporary.

Okay, so now you know which styling products you need to use. Now for some styling tips so you get the most from them.

Less is best. Avoid using too much styling product, and you'll avoid having a greasy mop for a hairdo. The amount you need depends upon hair type, length and the style you want. It's worth

101

remembering that you can always add more, but you can't take it away, so be sparing and apply carefully. There's no point just splodging a huge blob on top of your head and hoping it'll end up in the right place. Much better to comb the product evenly through wet hair from a blob on the palm of your hand. If only one or two locks need disciplining, then apply the product to dry hair, using your fingertips to put it just where you want it.

Be selective There's no need to use a cocktail of styling sprays, mousses and gels, unless you want hair like cardboard or an empty purse. Most work fine on their own.

Applying the heat
You now have a perfect understanding of styling products – but what about heated stylers that go with them? Lo! An at-a-glance guide:

Hairdryers dry your hair (yep, we all know that) but used with a combination of brushes and attachments they will help curl or straighten your hair too.

Curling tongs on long, dry hair make tight, spiral curls. Brush gently to give your hair luxurious waves.

Crimpers sandwich dry hair between two heated plates for the crinkle-cut-chip look.

Bendy rollers give soft curls and may be easier to use on short hair. Heated ones are most effective. Use them on dry hair, and make sure you wind them as instructed on the pack.

Heated rollers are most effective on shoulder-length hair to form bouncy curls. No good on short hair because it won't wrap round the roller, and ineffective on

Curling Tongs

long hair because the sheer weight of your tresses will soon pull the curls straight.

Diffuser drier attachments which resemble satellite
television dishes are used with bog-standard hairdryers to gently dry curly hair. The result is bouncy, well-shaped curls with lots of body.

Root lift attachments use plastic 'fingers' to give lots
of lift to the roots of straight hair. Attachments are made to fit onto standard hairdryers.

For the sake of your hair's health it's important to
know what you're doing with heated stylers. Over-heating your hair will cause it to dry and split. Remember that your scalp is very sensitive, so it too deserves the gentle touch.

Hold the hairdryer 12 inches (30cm) away from your head.

Always use the lowest heat-setting possible. It may take longer to dry your hair, but your patience will be rewarded with lovely locks and untraumatised hair.

Point your hairdryer slightly downward as you use it. The stream of warm air will smooth the surface of each hair making it look shiny. Your hair will be stronger and less prone to damage.

Try not to use heated stylers every time you wash your hair. Be especially careful with tongs, crimpers or heated rollers which come into direct contact with your hair. Whenever possible let your hair dry naturally in the big outdoors.

Brushes and combs

The longer your hair, the more important it is to use a good brush and comb, and to know the correct technique.

When you brush your hair don't forget to tip your

head upside-down to do the underside. Brushing doesn't just smooth your hair: it loosens dirt and dandruff, massages your scalp and spreads your hair's oil over its entire length. This oil makes your hair shine, and improves its suppleness making it stronger.

Never brush wet hair – it will 'stretch' each strand

making them vulnerable to damage.

Don't overdo it. A quick brush through in the morning is all

your hair needs. If you do it too much your hair will get greasy quickly, and you increase the risk of damaging it. Anyway, who has the time to brush their hair morning and night 100 times?

Brushing up on brushes and combs

◎ Rubber-backed brushes allow the brush to move through your hair with the minimum risk of snagging, and massage your scalp as you use it.

★ Paddle brushes have a wide, square head and short bristles; perfect for long hair.

◎ Bristle brushes spread the natural oils through your hair so that it looks ultra-shiny.

★ Ventilated brushes are used with hairdryers. The holes in the body of the brush allow hot air to escape so that your hair doesn't get too hot.

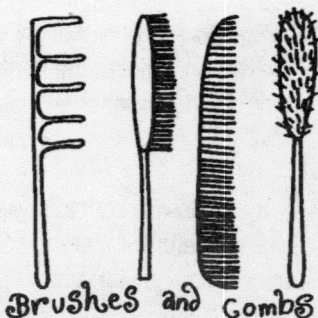

Brushes and Combs

🌀 Radial brushes have a round body that lets you style curls into your hair when used with a hairdryer.

★ Choose a wide-spaced, round-toothed comb which will move through your hair without snagging.

🌀 Only use a comb on wet, conditioned hair.

★ Comb short hair with your fingers to get extra body and lift.

🌀 Comb long hair in three stages to avoid knotting and pulling it. Start by combing the bottom section, then comb from the middle to the ends, and finish by combing down the entire length.

follicle fun

erms, relaxers and colorants all use chemicals to change the appearance of your hair, either permanently (that is, until the chemically-treated hair grows out) or temporarily. You need to think carefully before committing, because any permanent chemical process damages your hair.

The chemicals used in both perming and relaxing, for instance, reduce the bonds in your hair, then re-link them so that each hair is a different shape. What's more, unless the process is carefully monitored, the bonds can be permanently destroyed and your hair will become brittle.

Perms – instant curls, full time
Although a perm will make curlers, crimpers and tongs obsolete, extra care and conditioning will be needed.

Permed hair has lots of body and curl when it is first done, but as it starts to grow out you are left with flat roots and curly ends. Making it look good becomes more and more time-consuming.

Relaxers – getting it straight
These are most often used to permanently straighten tight, curly hair. Get a professional to do it; in the wrong hands you risk broken hair and a burnt scalp. Regrowth is a problem, as is loss of condition.

Colour – gilding the lily
It is possible to colour your hair without damaging it, and some colorants contain conditioners to make your hair really shiny and silky. There are three types of hair colorant:

Temporary rinses last for one to three shampoos, and the results are quite subtle – usually warming and enhancing your natural colour. They make your hair very shiny and do no damage.

Semi-permanent dyes last from six washes to six weeks, and give a more intense colour than temporary rinses. You cannot use them to lighten your hair.

Permanent dyes last until the colour grows out. You can achieve almost any colour you like, but any process which involves lightening your hair will cause some damage, leaving it drier and prone to split-ends. Those who opt for permanent colouring, especially when the difference between the natural colour and dye is great, accept that recolouring will be necessary once the hair starts to grow.

Highlights only lighten sections of hair to mimic how it would look in the sun. Highlights use a permanent colouring process which can look very natural, and root regrowth is barely noticeable.

Spray-on lighteners (or even lemon juice rinses) are frowned upon by hairdressers because they can do lots of damage. A conventional hair lightening process involves chemicals to lighten your hair colour, followed by a chemical that stops the process when the desired shade is achieved. A process which doesn't feature this second step means you have no control over the final colour, and it may leave your hair extremely dry and brittle.

You can use temporary and semi-permanent colours at home, but it is safer to have permanent colour, relaxers and perms done by a professional. It takes a lot of experience to judge the exact effect the chemicals will have on your hair. With a botched home job, your hair could resemble a patchwork quilt; curls could sprout geyser-like; and relaxed hair become stressed to breaking point.

The point of all this advice is to look before you cut, and think before you curl. Don't fill a boring Saturday afternoon with a mad, impulsive session in the bathroom. Much better to take your time, get good advice and really enjoy follicle fun. So let's raise our wide-toothed combs and gentle brushes to happy, healthy hair.

chapter 6
Making-up made easy

...what to buy
...how to use it

he first time you wear make-up is likely to be in the privacy of your own bedroom, with no-one but your threadbare teddy to witness the event. Sheer eagerness to see what you'll look like will make you grab whatever's to hand, and with indiscriminate fingers you'll set about slapping it on. But when it comes to wearing it in public, finger-painting your face is not good enough. This chapter is all about making you a make-up maestro.

It doesn't take long to realise that make-up can transform your face, making your eyes and lips look bigger. The first time you see yourself in bright red lipstick and lashings of mascara can come as a bit of a shock. Trouble is, it'll also come as a shock to everyone who knows you. The classic parental response as you tip-toe down the hall, trying to avoid detection is: 'You're not going out like that, young lady.' For when it comes to teenage make-up, you can't wear just any old daub.

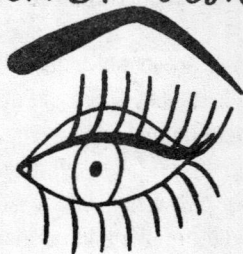

Why are you wearing make-up?

The following reasons are not valid: it's fashionable, your friends wear it, you were given some for Christmas, it came free with a magazine. Wear make-up if: it flatters your features and makes you feel good. If you don't think make-up is doing you any favours, then do without it.

The right stuff

Most people start by sneaking their mum's or older sister's make-up. However, what's right for your mum or big sis may not be right for you. For a start, their colouring and skin type may differ, and secondly, the palette of colours used by older folks does not suit bright, young things. So, as soon as you feel that make-up and you are going to get along, you need to buy a few colours of your own.

Where and when to wear it

Okay clever clogs, so you know it goes on your face. But it is also important to understand that you don't have to wear make-up all the time. If you wear it for special events, then the ritual of doing your face becomes special in itself. If you wear make-up round-the-clock, you'll end up feeling undressed without it, and it won't be special at all. Use it only when you want to knock 'em off their feet.

There are lots of times when you just can't wear make-up -- at school, for instance. Sport and make-up never really go together because you sweat it off. And you can't wear make-up in bed, despite the impression given by Hollywood films, because it makes a vast mess of your pillowcase, you wake up looking like a panda, and it is a mean and rotten thing to do to your skin.

Forget the painted face routine

Fashions in make-up change from season to season. If you look in magazines you'll see that trends in lip shades, brow shapes and make-up colours are changing constantly. So, when it comes to putting together your first make-up kit, don't worry about being the very pinnacle of all that is fashionable, for tomorrow it will be old hat. Natural-looking make-up is always flattering on teen complexions. Strong shades are too overwhelming and hard to apply because they show up mistakes. The so-called 'barely-there shades' have only been available for a few years, and they really are the best thing since sliced bread when it comes to teen make-up kit.

'Barely-there' (or translucent) shades for eyes, lips and cheeks look strong on the palette, but when you apply them they are soft and subtle – a sort of watercolour effect. They enhance your features, yet you can hardly see that you're wearing make-up. People, guys more specifically, see the real you, looking somewhat gorgeous, not a painted face.

These shades are very easy to apply because you only need to use a little, and they blend easily and naturally with your skin tone. Should you need further convincing, may I point out that this make-up has boys (and even parents) fooled every time. If you wear barely-there shades they'll be dumbstruck by your enhanced loveliness, but will fail to realise that you are, in fact, wearing make-up.

the basic make-up kit

here are hundreds of different brands, thousands of products and squillions of shades of make-up around. To make the job of buying easier it's a good idea to set a budget, and to write a list of the products you want, and what you want them to do.

Applicators: finger-painting your make-up is just not good enough. Would the 'Mona Lisa' have looked as beautiful if Da Vinci had finger-painted it? No, so invest, as did Da Vinci, in some soft brushes. Make-up brushes make it easy to blend colours smoothly and evenly. For a basic kit you'll need: a concealer brush, foundation sponge, powder pad, lip brush, blusher brush and a couple of eye shadow applicators.

★ Concealer: covers up spots and dark circles. Choose a shade slightly lighter than your natural skin tone (always check the tester on the back of your hand and look at it under natural light). Apply with a clean concealer brush, then blend onto your skin until the edges are invisible.

◎ Foundation: creates a smooth, even-coloured base on which to apply make-up colours. It shouldn't be used to create a three-inch thick mask, so apply it sparingly with a damp cosmetic sponge. Choose a shade that matches your skin tone, and apply it all over your face, including your eyelids. Pay extra attention to your chin and hairline as tell-tale smudges will give the game away in an instant. If you think a foundation is too heavy, try a tinted moisturiser.

★ Loose face powder: stops your skin from shining and sets the base. Choose one that's translucent, rather than one that will change your skin colour leaving you with a face several shades pinker than your neck. Apply with a powder pad, gently pressed onto your skin.

⊙ Eye shadows: emphasise and shape your eyes. Look out for colour co-ordinated duo packs (most come with applicators) and if you are not sure which colours to buy, start with browns – they suit everyone! First apply the lightest shade over your eyelids and up to your brows. Next apply the darker shade (remembering that less is best) following the line of the eye sockets to the outer corner of your eyes to give a shadow effect.

★ Eye liner: worn above your upper lashes to make your eyes look bigger. You can use an eye-liner pencil, which gives a very fine line but is quite tricky to apply, or a kohl eye-liner pencil which is easier to use, but gives a soft, smudgy line.

⊙ Mascara: the most effective way of drawing attention to your eyes. If you are only going to buy a couple of make-up bits, mascara and lipstick are the ones to get. Black is the most popular mascara colour because it looks the most natural, co-ordinates with all make-up shades, and has the most dramatic effect.

To apply stroke the wand over your top lashes, from root to tip. Repeat for the lower lashes. Allow a couple of minutes to dry and apply a second coat. Keep the wand clean as this will make it easier to extend the lashes evenly. Blobby mascara is a no-no. There are moisturising, waterproof, smudgeproof and non-waterproof mascaras – choose the

Eye Shadow

Highlight

mirror

Shade

EYE LINER

MASCARA

LIPS
fill in / outline

Blot with tissue.

one which suits your lifestyle. If you opt for waterproof mascara, buy a good eye make-up remover.

★ Lipstick: pick a colour that you like, bearing in mind that darker shades look better against dark skin, while pale skin is flattered by lighter, pinker shades. Apply with a lip brush; it gives a more even, precise coverage and lasts longer. Start by drawing round the outline of your lips. Follow your natural lip-line exactly – redrawing it to make your mouth look larger or smaller takes lots of practise. Even when well-executed it is obvious, so don't bother. Then fill in your lips, again using the lip brush. Finally, blot with a tissue by placing it between your lips and gently pressing them together.

◎ Blusher: use a tiny amount to give your complexion a healthy glow. Too much blusher and you'll be stopping traffic.

Wear it on top of your cheekbones to make your face look wider and longer; below your cheekbones to make your face look thinner. Blusher brushed on the 'apples' of your cheeks (the soft, round bits that appear when you smile) looks natural because this is where the colour shows when you blush.

Make-up kit extras

If this make-up lark is really your bag and you feel confident that you are using make-up for the right reasons, build up your basic kit with these little luxuries.

◎ Eye brow pencil: to shape and define your brows. Available in a variety of colours from blonde to black.

114

★ Eye lash curlers: look like an instrument of extreme torture, but are, in fact, easy and painless to use. Simply clamp the curler round the roots of your lashes, hold for a few seconds, then release. The result is longer-looking lashes. You may never need to use mascara again.

☻ Eye lash dye kits: for those with fair lashes who don't want to faff around with mascara. You have to keep your eyes closed throughout the process so you will need the help of a steady-handed friend. Most beauty salons offer this service.

★ Clear mascara: if you are blessed with thick, dark lashes or only wish to tinker with nature a little, then clear mascara is for you.

☻ Cream blusher: harder to apply than powder, and not the best for oily skin, but it has greater staying power and more intense colour than powder blushers.

★ Lip pencil: use it to create a strong line round your lips, before using lipstick. Lip pencils used alone will give you a long-lasting, matt lip colour.

☻ Lip gloss: makes your lips look really shiny. Use it on its own or on top of matt lipstick.

Where and how to get the best

A big chemist with lots of choice is the best place to start looking for make-up. First of all wander around and go 'wow' a few times in the face of the huge selection of stuff that's on offer. Armed with your list of desirables boldly go up to the counter and let the assistant tell you everything you want to know. Cosmetic

115

Cosmetic Assistant
sue
TESTERS
THE CHEMIST

counter assistants are usually specially trained (albeit by one cosmetics manufacturer or another) and they can help you find exactly what you want. Use their knowledge and their testers (for hygiene purposes test on the back of your hand, not on your face), but don't be intimidated into buying something you don't want. If it all becomes too confusing, tell the assistant you're going to have a herbal tea and a good think. Use this time to look at the colours you have tested under daylight, to make sure nothing is irritating your skin, and that you are sticking to your list and budget. Once you are sure about what you want, head back to the shop and lash out with your cash.

putting it on...

ractise, practise, practise in front of an evenly-lit mirror, then double-check the strength of the colours under daylight. The first time you put on make-up it takes ages; you end up with one eye that looks twice as big as the other, and a lip line that's heading off toward your right ear. But with practice you'll soon be a dab hand. Copy make-up ideas from magazines and decide if they're right for you or not. Whatever the result, have fun putting it on and wearing it – because that's when make-up works best.

Learning how to wear make-up is one thing. Taking it off is another. Most

make-up is easily removed with cleanser or soap and water, but mascara is harder to budge. You need to buy a specially-formulated oil or cream product which you apply with cotton wool, using gentle, downward strokes over your lashes. Don't try scrubbing around your eyes with soap and water – this skin is very delicate. What's more, you risk getting soap in your eyes. Ouch! Most importantly, have a routine for removing make-up and stick to it religiously. Promise yourself never go to bed with your make-up intact, and that you will remove it as soon as it has served its purpose.

eye brows

o pluck or not to pluck, that is the question. The finer your brows are, the more 'open' your face looks. Even the angle of their curve counts; a subtle curve looks soft, while a high arch looks more sophisticated. Tapered and tamed brows look best with make-up, and make you look very well groomed.

117

If you decide to pluck your eyebrows, follow these really easy rules to make it as successful – and painless – as possible.

1 Decide what you want to do. You may only want to remove a few stray hairs at first, but if you decide to go for a total reshape, it's worth copying from a picture and having a mate round to give your plucking the critical once-over.

2 Do it at least 24 hours before a special occasion; plucking can leave your skin red.

3 First, steam your face over a bowl of very hot water. This opens your pores and makes plucking less painful.

4 Use tweezers to remove each hair one-by-one. Only remove hairs from beneath and between your brows; taking them from above will spoil their natural line.

5 Finish one brow, then do the other one to match. Be very careful as each hair can make a big difference to the finished look. Don't be rash, take it slowly and keep an eye on your progress.

If you don't like the finished result, don't panic. Eyebrows do grow back, and it's only after continual plucking that regrowth may cease.

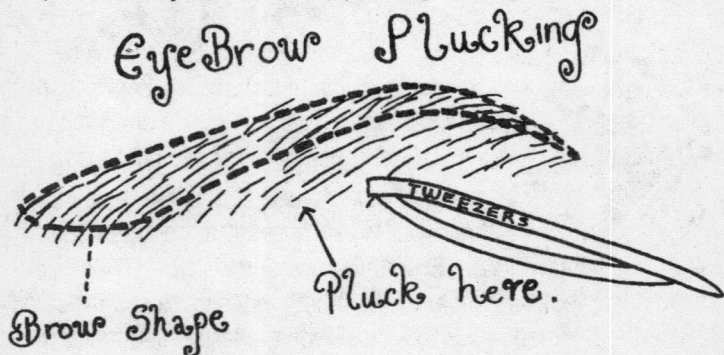

Eye Brow Plucking

TWEEZERS

Brow Shape

Pluck here.

burning make-up questions

kay, so you don't go to bed worrying about which lipstick to wear. Maybe thoughts about exams and assessments are uppermost in your mind. However, in case you are wondering, here are the answers to the most asked make-up questions.

"Does it make you spotty?"

Make-up itself can't cause spots, but wearing heavy, oily bases can aggravate them. It's best to choose water-based foundations, or those labelled 'non-comedogenic', which means they won't block your pores.

"What about sensitive skin?"

Skin can be sensitive to all sorts of ingredients in cosmetics, and unless you know precisely which ones cause you grief it can be tricky to find the right range. However, any range that is labelled 'hypoallergenic' will be free of common irritants and suitable for most sensitive skins.

"What make-up should I take out with me?"

You don't want a suitcase full of colour in tow, so pare your palette to the minimum. The best touch-up kit consists of lipstick, face powder and blusher. Pack a small mirror, and brush or comb as well. Take a concealer stick for spot repairs.

"What's waterproof mascara?"

A waterproof mascara will stay put while you swim, sob or shower but it has to be taken off with an oil-based remover. Smudgeproof mascara will withstand normal wetness round the eyes though a flood of tears will leave you looking like a panda. Use a normal eye make-up remover.

perfume

Fragrance is the make-up you can't see, and its scent lingers in the mind, long after you've left. That doesn't mean that perfume is a replacement for hygiene. You can't mask the odour of smelly armpits with it, so have a wash and wear deodorant as well. Fragrance is available in different strengths, with prices to match. The stronger it is, the longer it lasts on your skin, and the less you need to use. Pure perfume is the strongest concentration, followed by eau de parfum, eau de toilette and, finally, cologne. Dab or spray it on your wrists and behind your ears.

Perfume pointers

◉ Try the fragrance on your own skin; perfumes smell differently on everyone. Wait ten minutes before buying.

★ Once you have opened the bottle, store it out of sunlight with the top firmly in place.

◉ Don't wear fragrance while sunbathing: it can stain your skin and cause a rash.

★ Don't reapply your fragrance just because you can't smell it anymore; your nose gets used to smells and ignores them after a while. A good fragrance will last for several hours.

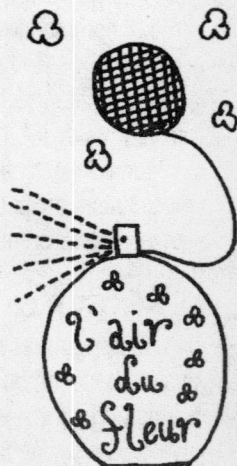

l'air du fleur

Making out, making-up, boys and you

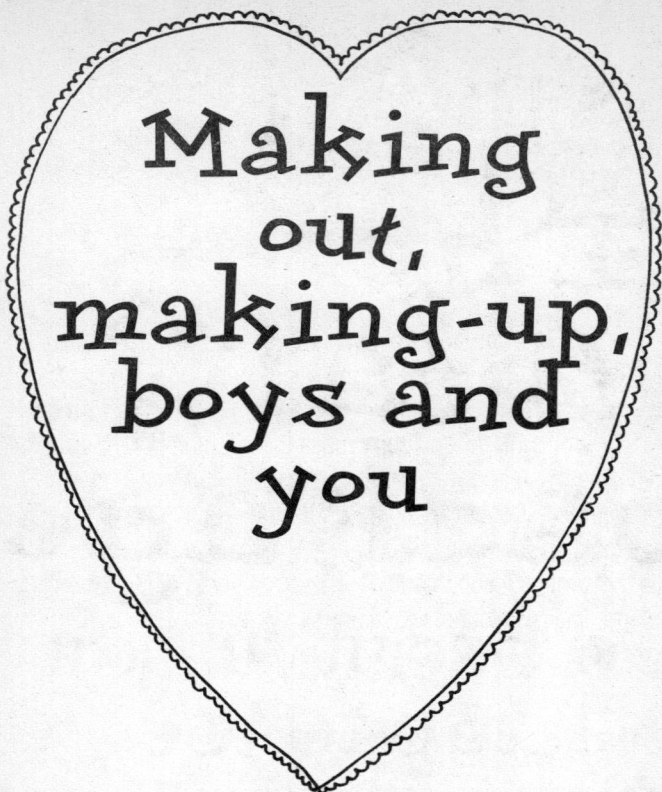

Most boys are completely put off by girls who wear too much make-up, so don't make the mistake of thinking that wearing loads of slap will make you the most attractive thing on earth. Boys worry about make-up for two reasons – first, because it makes you seem untouchable and they're terrified it's going to end up all over them in a snog-up situation; and secondly, a lot of boys feel they're not talking to the real you, but to a painted face. Don't get into the habit of thinking you're not worthy of being seen without lipstick, or go into a wild panic should he happen to see you minus mascara. Boys just aren't into the complexities of lip-lining, shadow-blending and lash-curling. They're far more interested in the real you. Nice to have some good news for a change, isn't it?

chapter 7

The total package

...a beautiful you
...top to toe

When you started this book you didn't know a brow brush from a witch's broomstick, a depilatory cream from a pint of UHT milk. Now look at you! You are a boffin of beauty, a scholar of skin care and a master of make-up. Award yourself a degree in gorgeousness. Congratulations!

Never again will you quake in fear of a spot, nor agonise over which bra to buy. There's no more confusion about conditioners, or bemusement about blushers; you are just straightforwardly sussed. Knowledge, dear reader, is power. While the contents of this book may not make you the next Prime Minister, it has hopefully given you some power over your own life, and the changes you are going through in this mad, bad and wonderful life-journey called teenage.

Change of any kind is daunting, but when it

involves your body, your appearance, and the way you think about things it can seem pretty scary. Actually, it's not. No matter how large your bust, how glam your hair cut, or which mascara you wear, at the end of the day you'll still be you.

The beauty industry is only too happy

to indulge us in our efforts to change those things we dislike about ourselves, and enhance those that we do. Unfortunately, some slip into the trap of thinking that if they use a certain shampoo, or skin care product, or go on a certain diet then they will become a better person. You can't get confidence in a bottle; being happy with the person you are on the inside is much more important than striving for physical perfection.

Even the most confident person

may dislike one or more of their features, but because they are basically happy and full of self-esteem, it's not a big deal.

Confidence
Self-Esteem

Happiness.

rules for a gorgeous life

Make self-esteem your number one beauty ideal. If you feel good about yourself, you can't help but be attractive. This doesn't mean you should walk round telling everyone you're gorgeous, but it does mean being really happy with who you are.

Understand the changes that your body is going through and look after it. A balanced diet and lots of exercise are both essential to teen health. Body confidence only comes about if you look after your whole self.

Dieting so that you're the minute size of a supermodel is not only unnecessary, it is very bad for you. Keep a firm grip on reality, and make feeling good a priority, not the pursuit of an unattainable image from a magazine (unless you happen to have a full set of studio lights, hairdresser, make-up artist and stylist in permanent attendance).

Have fun experimenting with the new looks you can achieve with hair and make-up products. If you feel like you can't face the world without six lipsticks and half a ton of hair gel, you've probably taken things a bit far. But if bright green eye shadow, purple blusher and pink hair make you feel good, then do it. (Can't guarantee that you won't get into trouble for it though.)

124

★ Don't let spots make your life a misery. They can be beaten.

◎ Don't be afraid to use your clothes, hair and make-up to make a statement. Clothes don't just cover your body, they also give out signals to others about the sort of person you are, or the sort of person you want to be. If you feel a day-glo pink mini says more about you than a pair of sensible trews ever can – and it's important to you that you make that statement – then go ahead, express yourself. Does it matter if you spend the rest of your life cringing every time your mum gets out the photo album, knowing that you and your screamingly-loud clothes are caught forever within its pages?

★ And here's a blast from the past – grooming. Be it ever so humble it does help your over-all, altogether gorgeousness if you sometimes clean your shoes, iron a shirt, replace a button and mend holes in your tights. See, I told you it was nostalgic, but that doesn't make it any less valid as a beauty tip.

◎ It is always worth remembering that as a teenager you are entitled to confidentiality when you see a GP. It doesn't matter whether you have gone to see them about acne or athlete's foot. Your local surgery may even run special teen clinics.

Enjoy yourself, this is the start of the rest of your life, so make an extra special effort to make your teen years the best so far.

Express yourself

Glossary

...at a glance beauty speak

(Check out this list and never be blinded by beauty science again!)

Acne: that wonderful (except it's not) condition that gives you spots. Blame it on your hormones.

Alcohol-free: contains no alcohol to dry the skin.

AHAs: Alpha hydroxy acids. Derived from fruit, they peel away the fine top layer of the skin's surface so that it looks smoother. Rubbing a banana on your face won't have the same effect, so don't try it.

Astringent: a toner for the skin, usually containing alcohol. Temporarily tightens pores and makes your skin feel cool and refreshed.

Biodegradable: means the product can be broken down by the environment, although how long it takes is another matter.

Botanical: to do with plants. Seen on the packaging of some products where plant extracts are used.

BUAV: British Union For The Abolition of Vivisection. This group campaigns against testing on animals, and awards rabbit logos to animal-friendly cosmetics.

Cellulite: dimpled fat on your body. It's completely harmless, but anyone who has it tends to hate it somewhat. A sensible diet and exercise are the best way to combat it.

Collagen: part of your skin that gives it structure and strength, and which, I regret to inform you, breaks down as you get older, which is why old bods' skin is saggy. Synthetic or animal-derived versions are added to cosmetics.

Comedone: posh word for a blackhead.

Conditioner: an after-shampoo treatment that smoothes the outer surface of each hair to leave it shiny and strong.

Cuticle: the posh name for that very same top layer of your hair which conditioner lays flat, funnily enough. Also the name for the skin that grows around the base of your nails.

Dandruff: flaky scalp caused by everything from micro-organisms to not rinsing your hair well enough.

Depilation: a posh word for hair removal methods, such as shaving, waxing and depilatory creams.

Dermatologically tested: tested to see if it's suitable for use on skin (I should hope so too). This term does not necessarily mean that a product is suitable for sensitive skins.

Emollient: a posh word for moisturiser. That's the beauty industry for you; just one posh word after another.

Exfoliant: that's right! Yet another posh word, this time describing a product which removes dead skin cells from the top layer of your skin.

Follicle: a pore from which hairs grow. We're covered in 'em, except for the follicle-free soles of our feet and palms of our hands.

Fragrance-free: a cosmetic that has not a sniff of fragrance in it. It's left out because some people are allergic or sensitive to it.

Free radicals: not, as the name suggests, a group of liberated forward-thinkers, but a term used to describe particular oxygen molecules within the skin that may be involved in skin ageing. It's thought to be environmental factors, like sunlight, which set them off.

Hydration: a posh word, yet again, for moisturising.

Hypoallergenic: contains as few ingredients as possible, therefore minimising the chances of allergic reaction. However, as there is always going to be someone, somewhere, who is allergic to something it's impossible to make a completely allergy-free product.

Keratin: the protein found in your nails, skin and hair.

Liposome: claimed to be a means of carrying skin care ingredients deeper into the skin. It has no skin conditioning properties itself.

Matt: not shiny and also the shortened version of the name Matthew, not that he's got anything whatsoever to do with beauty-speak.

Melanin: the colour pigments in the skin that give you a tan.

Micronised: a term used to describe particles in make-up that have been ground. These tiny particles give make-up a smooth finish. Sure beats putting lumpy porridge on your face.

Moisturiser: simply stops your skin from losing moisture so that it can be all soft and supple.

Non-comedogenic: products which won't clog your pores; seen on products for oily skin.

Organic: to do with living plants and animals. Much favoured, but much abused word among some cosmetics manufacturers.

PABA: a chemical sunscreen. Some people are allergic or sensitive to it, so some sun products are labelled 'PABA-free' if they use an alternative chemical sunscreen.

pH adjusted: made to match the natural, slightly acidic, pH of your skin. Don't panic if your cosmetics don't make this claim; skin is quite capable of adjusting itself.

Pores: the holes in your skin that vent sweat and sebum. You can't see them unless you have open pores in oily areas of your skin.

Sebum: the oil that your skin produces in order to keep your hair and skin supple, and therefore strong and healthy. Your skin starts to produce more sebum during puberty. It's linked to spots.

Self-tanning lotion: contains a skin dye that acts upon the top layer of skin cells to make you look tanned. The effect lasts for around three days.

Skin tint: instant tan-in-a-bottle that washes off.

SPF: Sun Protection Factor. The level of protection, from SPF1 to SPF25, against UVB rays offered by sunscreens. Just remember folks, the greater the number, the greater the protection.

Sun block: the highest level of UVB protection available.

Thickening mascara: makes your eye lashes look fuller. Doesn't mean the mascara gradually solidifies in the tube.

UV protection: if a product offers this without giving an SPF number, you can't be sure that the level of protection is sufficient for your needs. Don't rely on it in the sun!

Volume: nothing to do with your personal stereo, everything to do with making your hair look fuller and more bouncy. The term 'body' means the same thing.

With natural extracts: some of the ingredients are from natural sources, but not necessarily all of them. Read labels carefully, nature lovers.